Sales Mixology

Why the Most Potent Sales and Customer Experiences Follow a Recipe for Success

PRAISE FOR
SALES
MIXOLOGY

"Michael Sherlock's second book, *Sales Mixology: Why the Most Potent Sales and Customer Experiences Follow a Recipe for Success*, is both innovative and inspired by common sense. These days, common sense is not so common, and that's what makes this book such a breath of fresh air! Michael has taken the lost art of positive customer experiences, conversations, and simple hospitality and re-introduced it in a format that is easy to relate to and teach throughout your organization. She illustrates how to tap into each team member's potential, lay out a common ground upon which to achieve their maximum potential through core value alignment, and re-introduces them to the lost art of conversation. This conversation technique will truly engage the customer and make them feel important and valued. I cannot wait to share this book with my team and introduce these ideas to improve our own customer experience!"

Denise Jerome
CEO of Michaelis Events, Speaker and Contributing Author of
Imagination@Work: Shifting Boundaries in the Modern Workplace

"Michael Sherlock had me hooked in the first chapter of this book! I normally wouldn't purchase a book about sales (or marketing), because I'm one of the countless millions who have a bit of fear and angst around those topics. But this book isn't at all intimidating.

Michael's message is heart-focused, highlighting the power of emotional intelligence in a work setting. The lack of emotional intelligence in the corporate world is a challenge for many. In fact, what Michael writes about is an environment I know many envision working in, yet never find. As an Empowerment Strategist (similar to a coach/mentor) and a trauma specialist, I work with clients on the power of experience over intellectual understanding. Michael shares the same message, only in terms of sales. I love that!

Our feelings matter, and that's true at ALL levels, from the customer all the way up to the owner. The world is tired of the hyper-focus on bottom-lines and profit margins. All people matter, and this book demonstrates how emotional intelligence can help create an atmosphere that will attract repeat customers. If you do it right, the customers will find you through word-of-mouth, and that's the most powerful form of advertising there is.

From the perspective of a trauma specialist (developmental and intergenerational trauma), I am confident that the epidemic levels of stress, anxiety, depression and even chronic illnesses will decrease when employers see and honor their employees as individuals with lives, ideas, feelings and needs. Toxic work environments are one of the leading causes of these epidemics, and *Sales Mixology* describes, in detail, an antidote. My thanks to Michael Sherlock for the introduction to a new genre that I've tended to avoid most of my life. Not anymore!"

Jennifer Whitacre
Empowerment Strategist and Host of the "Yes, And…" Podcast

"I just finished my read of *Sales Mixology*. It was a delicious! The expression might not mean much to you, but well, I am French after all, and out of cooking school, before starting my retail career. I enjoyed every bit of this book. It is such a smart read, and it really refreshed my view of customer service and how to always try to reach perfection, by any means necessary! I am eager to share this book with my staff, my retail friends and my superiors. English is not my first language, but Michael Sherlock's book was an easy and smooth read. Each sentence makes you want to read the next, and I believe this is an excellent quality for a writer. Jane's experience at Fred's is described with a beautiful choice of words, and made me feel like I was living it. Michael Sherlock you hit the mark with this new book!"

Virginie Qader de Potter
Store Manager at The Walking Company Holdings, Inc.

"Michael does a great job painting a picture with her story telling. I was transported to Fred's and the training session with a good level of detail. And more importantly, she sums up the customer service principles so well that it feels very relatable. I can easily see how this relates to my own work environment. I didn't want to stop reading!"

Jessica (Cukrowski) Schnacky
Office Manager at Dr. Jennifer Orthodontics

Sales Mixology

Why the Most Potent Sales and Customer Experiences Follow a Recipe for Success

MICHAEL SHERLOCK

SILVER TREE
PUBLISHING

DEDICATION

It all began many years ago. I was meeting friends for happy hour at a place known for amazing cocktails. But when we sat at the bar, we were summarily ignored for several minutes while the bartender played on his phone. When he finally came over to us, his first question was *"What can I get you to drink?"*

I was put off by his brusque nature. After all, we went there to have a cocktail *experience*, not to *have a drink*. Determined that my cheerful demeanor would win out, I asked, *"What do you suggest?"* What followed was a series of disappointing interchanges that finally resulted in each of us getting a beautiful and delicious cocktail. None of us ever went back again.

A few years later, I began to chronicle my adventures in a blog called *A Cocktail a Day*. I highlighted examples of excellence, where both the cocktail *and* the experience were overwhelmingly positive. The cocktail, as the medium, has resonated well with people.

Today I seek out spectacular customer experiences in many industries. I write about them in my blog (www.ShockYourPotential.com), use them for inspiration for my podcast (www.ShockYourPotential Podcast.com), and as a vehicle for my #SecretShopperMichael persona.

When I am the recipient of a fantastic customer experience, I leave a specially designed folded business card with the person, letting them know that I recognized their efforts. These people often become the focal point of my blog, and I enjoy making sure their employers know that they have a quality team member.

I dedicate this book to every person who works hard to ensure others have meaningful and positive customer experiences. It takes effort, dedication, and leadership to infuse an entire company with positivity.

The customer may not always be right, but it is always right to deliver an exceptional customer experience.

TABLE OF CONTENTS

FOREWORD

When I first met Michael Sherlock, I was immediately fascinated by this colorful woman with pink hair and fabulous shoes — discussing, with a quiet authority, some of the most pressing issues that all managers tackle every day.

At the time of its release, her first book, *Tell Me More*, became mandatory reading for anyone managing people in the organization I was leading. By subtly empowering team members to solve their problems by guiding them to the solution with the right questions, Michael Sherlock put the most valuable resource of all organizations front and center: empowered employees.

With *Sales Mixology*, she takes this simple, yet brilliant, concept one step further. To be truly empowered to do the right things for the customer, and ultimately the company, every employee must be trained and, more importantly, allowed to be AGILE!

By breaking the old silos of expertise and specialization, with all the barriers that come with them, the empowered employee can and will jump in and put the customer experience first, even before their duty. It presupposes a comprehensive training in the company's purpose, not just in one's job description. But most importantly, it demands a culture where this agility is not only allowed, but also expected!

As a manager, I have always tried to package any information compellingly. Very often, organizations know what their message needs to be, but their delivery is lacking. Michael Sherlock's approach is a breath of fresh air in the management book world. Her novelist writing style has an incredible impact on the reader, who learns while enjoying a story. This book reads like a Michael Connelly novel, with minute-yet-riveting attention to detail when setting up the characters and the storyline. The result: the only thing that will slow you down may be the constant urge to stop and take notes to pass on to your clients or colleagues. I opted to immerse myself in Michael Sherlock's world and saved the note taking for the second (and soon third) reading.

Sales Mixology strikes the right chords and delivers the expert skills to create a cocktail of new approaches to your company or team culture. Read it responsibly: with haste and repeatedly!

Michael Dahan
Founder of Retail Answers Consulting, *Helping retail organizations face today's challenges of an industry in rapid transformation*

PROLOGUE
Full Circle – Maria's Perspective

On a cold November morning, Maria walked in the door at the convention center along with thousands of other women, and a handful of men. She was only a participant this year at the 13th Annual Women's Conference. The growth in her company, EyeSeeYou, kept her hopping all over the country with no time left for volunteering. She couldn't believe how far they'd come in a year.

She bent down to pick up a brochure that had fallen from her bag when she saw a crazy pair of neon green shoes with purple sequins walk up. With a giant smile, Maria stood up, smiling at Jane Smith.

"I was hoping I'd find you before the day got started," she said, smiling and giving Jane a big hug.

"Me too!" said Jane. "I've got about ten minutes before I have to check in with the speaker's lounge. You look great. How is everything?"

"Jane, I can't believe how great this year has been, and I can't believe that it's been a year since I met you. The company is doing fantastic.

"We are blowing our revenue budget entirely out of the water, and my reorganization has been seamless. My people are achieving heights they never knew possible, all because of something that woke me up last year at this time. I cannot tell you how thankful I am that I met you!"

Jane smiled at the praise but, in her usual manner, deferred the compliment. "Maria, I just gave you a tool. You chose to use it. I have something for you," Jane said as she pulled a book from her bag.

It was a hard copy of a book, Sales Mixology — *Why the Most Potent Sales & Customer Experiences Follow a Recipe for Success*, by Jane Smith.

"Jane! You got it finished!"

"Yep. I didn't have it done in time for submission for this year's conference, but I'm certainly going to plug it!" Jane said with a smile. "I wanted you to have the first official copy. I think you will enjoy it!"

Maria laughed as she took the book.

"Really, Jane? You think I'll like it? Tell Me More!"

Note to the Reader

Throughout *Sales Mixology*, you'll find endnotes that refer you to the "Inspiration" section at the back of the book, starting on page 183. In this special section, I share clarifying points, notes about my inspiration for the content in the book, and some *Thoughts from the Coffee Table* vignettes that originally appeared on my blog at *ShockYourPotential.com/Blog.*

Chapter 1

WHAT MAY I CREATE FOR YOU?

Jane Smith checked into The Prenton Hotel[1] in Belfast, Northern Ireland,[2] around 10:00 a.m. on a chilly Sunday in November. The sun was shining brightly, but she could see clusters of dark clouds throughout the sky. She wasn't expecting much in terms of glorious weather.

Traveling overseas was always tiring. A long overnight flight, coupled with an 8-hour time change, created a rather mind-numbing state. Nonetheless, Jane was excited to be there.

She had been hired to speak at a sales conference the upcoming Friday, presenting her *Tell Me More* leadership principles to more than 4,000 professionals in the spa industry. Owners, managers, and treatment providers would be in attendance. She had never been to Northern Ireland, and although her husband couldn't join her on this trip, she decided to make a whole week of it.

The hotel already had a room waiting for her, and she gladly embraced a rare morning nap.

That afternoon she explored the city by foot, wandering the cobblestone streets with a sense of wonder. She enjoyed a bowl of chowder at a small pub with a massive roaring fire. She was in heaven.

While she ate, she plotted out her next couple of days, knowing that a Black Taxi tour and the Titanic museum were on her must-do list. But she also knew that she didn't want to overdo it on her first day while battling time changes. That could be a recipe for disaster.

She spent the rest of the afternoon wandering, looking in store windows. She found a small neighborhood park where she was able to sit for a bit and watch children at play. One of Jane's greatest travel joys was to see how much life in other countries was similar to life in her own country. Just as the children in her native Seattle broke free from the confines of school on a rainy, drippy day, so too did these children seem ready to burst with pent up energy once let out.

Finally, Jane wandered back to her hotel, aware that jet lag was going to set in soon.

Deciding to keep the evening simple, she took the concierge's suggestion that she enjoy Fred's Jazz & Cocktail Lounge[3] in the hotel. The threatening skies had finally turned to bitterly cold rain, and staying in seemed like a good idea. Jane could have a light meal, enjoy some music, and then release her exhaustion to the giant soaking tub and enormous comfy bed. The concierge also told her that Fred's had one of the most impressive cocktail menus around, which piqued her interest.

Walking into Fred's was like stepping back in time. Deep red velvet-covered chairs and red leather couches dotted the landscape.

The dark wood walls gave a sense of warmth and beauty that made Jane wonder if she was dressed appropriately.

Part of the fun traveling in Northern Ireland, so far, had been people's complete acceptance of her wildly colored hair. Surprising hair colors were one of her trademarks. Currently white blond with deep purple roots, she felt royal inside the walls of this velvety cocktail lounge.

She sat at the bar. She always sat at the bar when she traveled.

Business travel could be lonely. Sitting at a bar allowed her to be around people, gaining a sense of community. She could engage or not, depending on how she felt. Jane also thought it unfair to be solo at a table, knowing a server could have two or more people, and thus an opportunity to earn a bigger tip.

The place was humming, alive with people and laughter and buzzing conversations. And from the bar, she could watch it all.

Despite the busyness of the bar, and what she was noticing looked like both a cocktail station and floor show, a bartender in a long leather apron, deep purple tie, and crisp white shirt came to her almost immediately. His warm smile was the first welcome.

"Welcome to Fred's. My name is Ken. I will take care of you tonight, along with my colleagues. May I ask your name?"

Jane was impressed, just by that alone. Sure, she had experienced similar welcomes before. Every time she went through Hartsfield-Jackson Atlanta International Airport, she often stopped at P.F. Chang's in Terminal A.[4] Their servers always asked your name, gave you theirs, and then placed a little tent card to remind you of their names. Once, out of curiosity, she picked up the card and flipped it over. "Jane" was written on the back, along with the words "club soda with lime." Brilliant!

She had been working on getting better at remembering names when meeting someone new. Sometimes her brain was a few steps ahead of her, letting the name to slip just past her awareness. It wasn't a trait she was proud of, but it was one she was determined to improve.

"Hello, Ken. My name is Jane."

"Welcome, Jane. Is this your first time at Fred's?" Ken asked and continued at Jane's smile and nod. "Wonderful! Would you allow me to give you a tour of our menu?"

"Absolutely! You make beautiful cocktails. I have no idea what to order."

"Jane, you are not alone. We have several wonderful and delicious concoctions. Let's find out what suits you best tonight."

Wow, thought Jane. *I am even more impressed!*

Jane hadn't considered that her dinner would become a learning opportunity, but it had already given her several key thoughts. First, she realized that, unlike the bartenders at P.F. Chang's, Ken did not write her name down, but he had repeated her name twice. That seemed significant and very similar to a strategy she was trying that prompts you to use someone's name three times in the first few minutes of an introduction.

Second, Ken's method of asking permission to give her a tour of the menu triggered something in her brain. And based on his last statement, she was wondering if he employed a similar strategy to her *Tell Me More* principles.

"Tour away Ken!" Jane said with a smile.

"Before I begin, let me ask you a couple of questions. Do you normally prefer a cocktail, beer, glass of wine, or something non-alcoholic?"

Jane was a little surprised by the question, if only because so often bartenders lead with house specials or their favorites to pour or mix. Sometimes they put a menu in front of you and walked away. That always felt so sterile.

"Great question, Ken. I like all the above depending on the circumstance. But I would like to start with a cocktail tonight."

"Excellent," Ken said with a smile as he flipped a few pages into the menu. "Now, some of the cocktails here are old favorites." He pointed to the first list. "Some are adaptations, and some are unique creations. But if there is anything that you would like that isn't listed, we can make that happen for you. As you can see," Ken swept his arm back to indicate an assortment of glass bottles and jars of all shapes and sizes, "we have an extensive supply of bitters, aromatics, syrups, herbs, and spices."

"Some days I feel more like a scientist than a bartender," he said, smiling.

Jane could understand that statement. The vials were large and small. Some had glass stoppers; some had eyedroppers; some had tiny spoons resting on top. Each drew her eye and interest.

It was at this point that Jane realized how many new people had arrived, and how much time she was taking with Ken. She felt guilty. He seemed to sense her unspoken discomfort and said, "Don't worry, Jane. Everyone will be well taken care of. Right now, you are my only customer."

Jane was shocked. He seemed to mean it. He had no sense of stress, and his focus was solidly on her. It was in that moment she noticed the addition of two more bartenders, greeting the new arrivals. It was like they magically multiplied to meet the needs of the guests.

Bringing her attention back to the menu, Ken asked another probing question. "Now tell me a bit about you. Are you partial to one kind of liquor over another? Or are there any liquors you don't particularly care for?"

Jane thought for a moment before she responded, not because she didn't have an answer, but because she was trying to fix his questions and their tone in her mind.

She'd been asked that question before, often with a bored slant as if the bartender were trying to cut down the list to get to a drink fast and easy. Ken, however, seemed to be using his questions, and her answers, to develop a profile from which he could launch solutions. It was very much like *tell me more*, but more direct.

"I am pretty daring," said Jane as she pointed to her hair. Ken nodded and smiled.

"I am currently a fan of rye whiskey, but I suppose the only thing I am not a fan of is Scotch. It tastes like drinking a leather couch."

That made Ken laugh heartily, and Jane smiled back.

"OK Jane, I hear you. You don't like peaty Scotch. Which makes it a great thing that you are in Northern Ireland and not Scotland." They both laughed while another staff member came to ask Ken a question. Instead of talking to Ken first, however, the staff member looked at Jane and said, "Please accept my apology. Would it be all right if I stole Ken for just one moment?" Jane was flabbergasted!

"Of course!" said Jane, feeling as if this question was very respectful. And before they left, Ken introduced the two.

"Jane, I would like you to meet Jacqueline. She is our Director of Training. Jacqueline, this is Jane. We are narrowing down her cocktail."

"Very nice to meet you," Jacqueline said, offering a hand to shake. "I promise only to steal Ken for a heartbeat."

Jane nodded agreement, and the two stepped over to the grand central station for mixology. They put their heads together, coming to an apparent agreement, and then Ken was back.

"Jane, I apologize for the interruption. Shall we continue?"

Through a series of other questions, Jane felt that Ken had her profile established. Then he knocked her socks off once again.

"Jane, there are several cocktails on our menu that I think you will enjoy. Tell me what you would prefer. Would you like to browse the menu on your own to decide? Would you like me to make some suggestions? Or would you like to trust me to make something unique just for you?"

That sealed the deal. There was only one choice, although Jane relished the fact that she was allowed to *make* that choice.

"Create away, Ken! My cocktail is in your hands."

And with that, Ken smiled, left her the drink menu to peruse and went in search of ingredients. When he returned with bottles and vials, stemware and a fruit bowl, a small kitchen blowtorch and chunks of raw sugar, Jane knew she was in for a treat.

Watching Ken create the cocktail, she could see his passion for the little things. She was sure this would be a rendition of an Old Fashioned, one of her favorites, but some of his ingredients were quite surprising.

From time to time he would glance up, smile, and then return to his masterpiece. It didn't take long, and yet Jane felt like she had been privy to a private show — a play just for her.

In the background, she could hear the band getting ready to start their set. The entire evening seemed perfect all the way around.

After the orange rind had been twisted, heated and rubbed around the rim of the glass, Ken presented her with the cocktail.

"I would suggest you let it sit for just a moment to settle the flavors and allow the ice to become one with the drink," Ken said, smiling because he saw how eager she looked to taste it.

"And of course, smell it. See if you can determine some of the flavors and distinguish the changes to the drink as they begin to blend."

Jane smiled, smelled, closed her eyes, and was impressed with the overall effect. When she finally gave in to her temptation to taste it, she savored the first notes on her tongue. Her smile was all Ken needed.

"I'm going to assume that means you like it?" Ken teased.

"Absolutely!" Jane replied. "This has been amazing so far. If the food is anything like this, I am in for a treat tonight."

"Yes, you are," replied Ken. "Would you like to see a menu right away, or would you like to enjoy this for a while?"

Jane loved this new question. It put her back in the driver's seat and gave Ken vital information without his having to make assumptions.

"Ken, I think I would like to enjoy this and the music for a bit first."

"Perfect Jane. Just catch my eye when you would like a menu."

Although she was engrossed in the music, she noted that Ken would often glance her way to see if she was ready to proceed with her meal. He was never intrusive and never neglected her. She wondered how he perfected that balance.

She had a wonderful meal and realized that she hadn't enjoyed an evening out quite as much in a long time. The whole experience got her brain buzzing with ideas. Every part of the evening provided her with other examples of excellence, and she jotted down notes on at least six cocktail napkins. It was getting absurd.

Just then, the band announced a short break. Ken was busy removing Jane's dinner dishes, and she was contemplating that giant bathtub and a full night of deep sleep when Jacqueline popped into her field of vision.

"Hello, Jane. How are you enjoying your evening?"

"Jacqueline, this has been lovely on so many levels!"

Jacqueline looked quizzically down at Jane's stack of impressive napkin notecards, making Jane laugh at the unspoken question.

"I suppose it's a hazard of the job," Jane said. "I'm a business writer and a speaker."

"Really?" Jacqueline said. "What do you write about?"

"I focus on leadership, sales, and customer experiences. And man, have I found the trifecta here tonight," Jane said with a smile.

"I'd like to know more about that. Do you mind if I join you for a moment?" Jacqueline asked.

"Please do!" Jane replied, enthusiastically. "Would you mind if I asked you a few questions?" Jane asked as Jacqueline made her way around the bar to take the seat next to Jane.

"Fire away."

"First of all, my experience here tonight has been exceptional. It has been an overwhelmingly positive customer experience. How do you make this happen?"

"Well Jane, before I answer that question, let me ask you one first. What is it about your experience that has made it so overwhelmingly positive?"

Jane had to laugh to herself. This was getting better every minute.

"Well, I suppose first, I have been blown away by the personal attention I have had from Ken, you and the entire team. This place is packed, and yet I feel like I am the only customer. How do you create that environment?"

Now it was Jacqueline's turn to laugh. "Great question, Jane. And I am so pleased to hear that we delivered our core promise to you. The cocktails, food, and music are all exquisite. But they mean nothing if we do not deliver an unforgettable personal experience."

Jane nodded in agreement. "I see what you mean. There are lots of places where I have enjoyed the food or the music or the cocktails, but not all of them draw me back again for another visit."

"Exactly," Jacqueline said, smiling. "That is my responsibility here with this team. I expect a lot out of them. But mostly I expect them to believe that it is vital that we deliver on that experience. I take a long time to make hiring decisions because I want to make sure we have the absolute right people."

"Wait," Jane said. "I don't want this to come out wrong, but I thought Ken said you were the trainer. Aren't hiring decisions made by the manager?"

Jacqueline smiled. "No offense taken. We do things a bit differently here, for a reason. See that woman over there by the kitchen?" Jane nodded when she saw the woman in a deep blue dress speaking with one of the chefs. "That is Sandra, the General Manager of the hotel. She is responsible for how the entire business performs. But she holds the rest of us responsible for the parts we play."

Jacqueline had to smile at Jane's confused look.

"Let me see if I can explain better using Fred's as an example. The Executive Chef is responsible for the quality of our menu, but his Sous Chef is responsible for making sure the kitchen runs smoothly every day to achieve that. The Director of Mixology is responsible for the variety and quality of our bar selections, but Ken, our Bar Lead, is responsible for making sure the bar meets all customer expectations. Both the Sous Chef and Ken screen candidates for their team, but I make the ultimate hiring decisions because I am responsible for making sure whoever we hire will be trained to meet our expectations. Does that make sense?"

It did, and Jane nodded, but she was surprised as well.

"I think I see where you are going here," said Jane. "The larger vision is held responsible at every level in the business. But at the end of the day, unless someone is willing and able to be trained, no matter their resume, you don't want them on the team. Is that right?"

Jane knew she was on to something when Jacqueline nodded before she finished her thought.

"Yes," Jacqueline said. "It means that we all must have a common vision and purpose. No one can be out just for themselves. They must see that we are trying to make something greater than just a meal or a cocktail or a night of great jazz. We all have to be committed to the single purpose of the overall experience. And that is expected by everyone throughout the hotel."

Jane was smiling and jotting more notes on napkins. Out of the corner of her eye, she noticed the General Manager walking toward Jacqueline. She was afraid she had already taken up too much time again, but neither woman seemed disturbed.

Jacqueline took the opportunity to introduce the woman. "Sandra, I'd like to introduce you to Jane. She is a business writer and speaker and has been enjoying how we do business here. She was picking my brain on a few things." Jane couldn't help but feel just a bit guilty. She hoped she wasn't encroaching on trade secrets. She said as much, and both women chuckled.

"No worries at all, Jane!" Sandra said with a giant smile. "We are very proud of what we do here, but there are no secrets. Just hard work, mutual respect, and a completely aligned vision."

"It certainly seems that way," Jane said, and then embarrassed herself with a yawn. That got both women laughing again as well.

"I am so sorry! I think the travel, time change, and great food has finally caught up to me. I hope you don't mind if I come back again tomorrow to observe and maybe ask some more questions," Jane said with a smile.

"We would be happy to have you again, Jane." Jacqueline said. "I am not sure what you have on your agenda tomorrow, but if you are available in the morning, I have a new hire training from 9:00 a.m. to 5:00 p.m. tomorrow. You would be welcome to sit in and observe for as much, or as little, as you would like." Sandra was nodding her agreement as well.

"I would love that!" Jane said. "What an offer!"

"Fantastic. Meet here in the bar at 9 o'clock sharp. I think you'll have fun."

As Jane said goodnight to both women and headed toward her room, she couldn't help but be excited about the opportunity in front of her. As she crawled into bed, she glanced at the stack of cocktail napkins with notes written on every inch of open space. She laughed and made a mental note to take her notebook with her tomorrow.

Chapter 2

DENNY THE DISHWASHER

Jane was up bright and early and decided to write in her journal while enjoying a cup of coffee in her room. She took the key points from her napkins, transferring them to her notebook. A nagging thought that wouldn't quite form buzzed in the back of her brain. But she was confident that, like puzzle pieces, they would start to come together once she laid them all out.

That was one of the core principles in her *tell me more* strategy. A big problem was simply a combination of many essential pieces of information.

To help find solutions to those big problems, Jane taught people to lay those pieces out, much like taking the items in a suitcase that is packed so full that even sitting on it can't get it to zip up. Then when you see all of the pieces individually, you are more likely to look at things from a different perspective. By "unpacking" the problem, and looking at the critical elements more objectively, the solution was often quite clear.

After a quick breakfast, Jane found herself outside the door of Fred's at 8:45 a.m. Jacqueline started chuckling when she came around the corner. "Eager for your first day at a new school, Jane?"

"You caught me. And I even brought you an apple!" Jane flourished a shiny green apple from her bag.

They both laughed while Jacqueline opened the door.

A restaurant is very different when no one is there. No sounds of dishes clapping against each other, no buzz of talk or laughter, no smells to delight and wonder the senses. It felt so alone compared to the vibrancy of the room the night prior, and she said as much to Jacqueline while she set up tables for her "students" that were about to arrive.

"I know what you mean, Jane. I used to feel the same way, but now I see it as a stage behind the curtain. The audience hasn't been allowed in yet, but they are eagerly waiting outside. The stage must be set properly, and the actors need to know their parts before that door should open. That's what I love about training days. It is our rehearsal for another performance."

That made sense to Jane. She liked the analogy. She tried to look at the room with a different perspective as several people filed in, and Jacqueline helped them to find a seat.

At precisely 9 a.m., Jacqueline called the group to order. Jane liked punctuality in meetings. It showed professionalism and became a contract of what people knew was expected of them as well.

"Welcome everyone! It is good to see you all. We have a full agenda day today, and every moment of your time has been planned to support your fast and smooth transition to our team."

She had all of their attention, and Jane felt a little giddy. This was fun!

"Although you have all been formally hired and are being paid for this day, I want each of you to think about today, and every day, as a daily job interview." People looked confused and a little uncomfortable. Jane had her suspicions of where this was leading and couldn't wait to see if she was right.

"When each of us, myself included, show up for work as if we were interviewing for our job, we will always bring our A-game. We will give our best each day to the team, the company and, most importantly, to the customer." People seemed to accept that answer but still looked uneasy.

"Every day, every one of us *IS* interviewing for our job. Perhaps for our current job; perhaps for a promotion. We are proving that we can, and will, do what is expected of us, and maybe even show more of what we can do. Our jobs aren't our rights; they are a privilege. And on this team, we owe it to ourselves and to our colleagues, to respect that privilege."

"Any questions so far?" Silence was the response. Jane had to hide a smile. Jacqueline had done just what Jane had anticipated. She set clear expectations. That could make people feel uncomfortable, yet anyone uncomfortable with clear expectations was probably not right for this team.

"OK. Here is what we are going to do today. I am going to go through our core business principles and expectations. This is going to require that you talk and interact. It is not enough for you to memorize these things and try to live by them. I must be confident that you can, and will, embrace them. No one leaves here today without talking." She smiled to take the sting out of the words.

"Lunch will be served to you by the kitchen team. You will also enjoy a wine-flight so that you can taste the impact on our menu by some of our signature wines." Everyone smiled at this, and Jane was both surprised and delighted by this unexpected twist.

"After lunch, you will each go with your department manager for training specific to your position. And we will wrap up together at 4:00 p.m. to debrief and work with tonight's team to prepare for doors open at 5:00 p.m."

Jane hadn't been sure she would stay the entire day but thought now that it might be worth pushing off the Titanic Museum one more day.

"Let's start with introductions. Please tell the group your name, your position, and the top reason that you think you are a perfect fit for the Fred's family."

Jane was intrigued by the group, which included a new bartender, a hostess, a dishwasher, a line cook, and six servers. What a diverse crowd to attend the same training! And why does the dishwasher need to know about the wine list, she wondered?

When Jacqueline got to her, Jane was stumped momentarily as what to say. "Hello. My name is Jane Smith. I am here to watch and learn about your training. I'm just a customer who is curious about how this place works." She said at last, with a sheepish smile.

"Thank you, Jane. I am so glad to have you join us! But today you aren't here to watch or listen. You are here to participate. And for today, you are a new barback."

When Jane looked confused, Jacqueline said, "Don't worry. I'll explain it as we go along."

Jane laughed nervously but smiled. OK! Barback it is!

"Let's begin. First, let me explain something unique about Fred's. We operate under the 'last person standing' principle." Jacqueline smiled at more confused looks from her audience, and yet Jane felt that she probably delivered this talk the same way each time for a reason. She knew that sometimes keeping your audience slightly off balance was a great tool for enhancing their message retention.

"This is what I mean. You will each know something about every position in the restaurant, and at times, be put in those other positions, to keep your skills sharp. We want you to have an appreciation for and understanding of everyone's job. It allows us to have better empathy towards the rest of our team. It also means that in times of crisis, or to hold off moments of crisis, someone can, and will, be in control. And one day that could be you." She turned to Jane, then to the dishwasher, and then to the bartender. Jane nodded in understanding.[5]

"Jane, I know you saw this in action last night. Do you know what I am referring to?" As Jacqueline was asking her the question, Jane was surprised that she did.

"Yes! When I first sat down at the bar, and Ken was giving me his full attention, I realized that a large group of people came in all at once. I was worried that Ken was spending all of his time with me, but suddenly there seemed to be several more bartenders." She triumphantly smiled while Jacqueline nodded in agreement.

"Precisely. I was certain you caught that. How do you think that happened, Jane?"

"Well, just from this little you've said so far, I imagine that you, or Sandra, moved people to the bar to ease the stress there."

"Nope," Jacqueline said with a devious smile. "Try again."

Jane turned her head to the side, pursed her lips, and gave a dreamy look. Jacqueline gave her a quiet moment to contemplate the answer while the others looked on, happy not to be the focus of the trainer yet.

In a flash, Jane knew the answer. "The *team* decided to go to help at the bar!" She knew she was right by the look in Jacqueline's eyes.

"That is exactly right, Jane. Our team is constantly looking, measuring, weighing, and balancing the needs of their responsibilities versus the good of the team for the benefit of the customer. In this case, two servers jumped in to help."

Wow, thought Jane. *That is impressive!* But it also made her wonder something.

"But if they were servers," Jane began to ask, "how could they fill in as bartenders?"

"Great question, Jane," Jacqueline responded. "They knew they wouldn't be responsible for making the drinks. They were there to greet customers, take orders, and help the bartenders and barbacks to deliver the drinks. Think of them as traffic control."

That made sense to Jane, and she nodded her understanding.

"Now let's hear from the rest of you. What do you think so far?" Like most groups of strangers, no one spoke up first. Jane admired Jacqueline's comfort with the quiet. It was a tactic she used often. But when no one volunteered, she began to pull people out of their comfort zone.

"Thomas, you are joining our bar staff, and I know you came from our most significant competition in town. What do you think about what I've talked about so far? Is this how you operated at Beldone?

Thomas wasn't necessarily uncomfortable being called on, but Jane reflected that it never seemed to be easy for the first person. "Well, no. I don't think we operated that way at all," Thomas said as if he were tossing the concept around in his head.

"Like here, we were often swamped, especially behind the bar. It's easy to get caught up in the demands of your job. I guess I can't imagine having the luxury of being able to have someone else help me out when I get in the weeds, much less have me be able to help someone else out in the kitchen or the dining room."

At Jane's confused look, Thomas said: "In the weeds is slang for being so crazy busy you are barely holding on." Jane smiled and nodded her thanks to the explanation.

"Thank you, Thomas," said Jacqueline. "Most places *don't* operate this way. And it is why we will train you differently. We have three core expectations:

- The customer, and their experience, *always* comes first.

- No one person or one position is more important than creating and maintaining an excellent customer experience.

- Each day you will be expected to find ways to deliver on our first promise, while also building the financial success of the company."

As she said the words, Jane watched the faces of those around her. Some seemed eager, some confused, and some looked bored. She had experienced the same in her meetings, so it wasn't unexpected.

She could tell that Jacqueline noticed the same. And like Jane would do herself, Jacqueline went first for one of the confused faces.

"Marcy, I see you look a little confused. What questions are running through your head?" Jane kicked herself for not bringing Jacqueline a copy of *Tell Me More*. She needed to remedy that at the break.

Marcy took a moment to gather her thoughts. "Well, I suppose it makes sense. But those are just three simple concepts. I'm not sure how they translate into the example that Jane gave about watching more people come to the bar last night."

"Marcy, that is a great comment. I'm so glad you made it," said Jacqueline with a slight grin. Jane felt like she was almost watching herself lead the group.

"So, let's break this down a bit. Marcy, the two people who jumped to the bar last night were both servers. One wasn't scheduled to clock in for 15 minutes, and the other only had one table already in her section. Why do you think they did what they did?"

"Hm. Well, I suppose that it was an easy enough decision for the server with only one table. She was on the clock and wasn't busy yet. If you have created this sense of taking care of each other, it would seem natural enough."

Jacqueline was nodding along, so Marcy continued. "But I have to be honest. I think it's great that the other server jumped in to help as well, but where I've come from, if you tried to clock in before your shift without approval from the manager on duty, that would get you in trouble."

Several heads around the tables were nodding in agreement, and Jane understood why.

"Marcy, why would you get into trouble? Tell me more." At these words, Jacqueline turned and gave Jane a little wink. Maybe she didn't need to bring her a book, after all, she thought while she gave a wry smile in return.

"Every place I've ever worked in was always trying to control costs. Even 15 minutes for one staff member above and beyond their scheduled shift can be costly. I would honestly be afraid to do that. People could be terminated for that, or at least written up." Marcy said this a little hesitantly, but her admission seemed to be just what Jacqueline wanted to hear.

"Marcy, I am so thankful for your honesty. Let me walk you through this using our three principles. I think it may make more sense then and give you some confidence in this. But I want to role-play it with you. Is that all right?" Marcy nodded agreement but didn't look too excited.

"OK, Marcy. The first principle is what?

Marcy read from the screen, "The customer, and their experience, *always* comes first."

"Perfect," said Jacqueline. "Pretend that you are the server who was not scheduled to clock in yet. Based on the first principle, and the scenario Jane experienced last night, what would make you comfortable clocking in early?"

"Well, when a large group comes in at once, I know that it is stressful and puts a lot of pressure on the bar. That can drag wait times to order and to get your drink. That would affect the customer experience. But,"

Jacqueline cut her off. "No 'buts' yet. Only reasoning and strategy allowed in this role play."

Marcy smiled and seemed to relax a bit.

"Now," Jacqueline continued. "Let's talk about the second principle. What about that one would make you comfortable clocking in early?"

"No one person or one position is more important than creating and maintaining an excellent customer experience." Marcy gave a thoughtful role of her eyes towards the ceiling and pursed her lips in thought. Jane noticed how everyone was paying attention now. This was so much fun!

"Well, I am assuming that everyone was hopping, so if the manager-on-duty wasn't free to make that decision, this principle would tell me it's all right to make this decision on my own, in this situation, because the benefits outweigh the negatives of 15-minutes of extra staff time." She was hesitant in her answer as she spoke, but Jane figured she was right on. Jacqueline's smile was proof.

"Excellent, Marcy. Does everyone else see where we are going with this so far?" People were nodding in agreement, and now more fully engaged.

"OK, Marcy. For the final round, talk us through the third principle." She made a "dunt-dunt-da" sound as if this were a game show. Even Marcy laughed at that as she answered again.

"Each day, you will be expected to find ways to deliver on our first promise, while also building the financial success of the company. This is a tough one, and the reason that I brought up the example in the first place. 'Financial success' can mean different things to different people and in various businesses. It still seems a gamble to me based on my history."

Jacqueline didn't let Marcy's answer divert her, but she knew when she needed to give Marcy a break from the spotlight. As she turned to the rest of the group, she said, "I think Marcy has done great so far. Who wants to jump in and help for our last principle?"

A couple of hands rose hesitantly, but Jane was surprised to see that Denny, the new dishwasher, raised his hand high and with confidence.

"Denny! What are your thoughts?" Jane held her breath. She wasn't sure what a dishwasher was going to know about this.

"Well, the way I see it is this. The cost per hour for the server is probably close to the cost for one or two cocktails. In that light, 15-minutes is nothing compared to the number of drinks you can serve to a large crowd, especially when they are happy." People began to nod, as did Jacqueline, indicating for him to continue.

"Then consider the rest of the people in the bar and the restaurant. I know I always groan when a large group comes in after me because I think it will affect my service, especially if I haven't ordered yet, or if I had just ordered." Everyone was nodding and agreeing., Marcy now seemed to see where he was going and agreed.

Feeling like he was the star pupil, Denny rose to his topic. "So, when you think about the commitment to continually look for ways to create an amazing experience while also impacting the bottom line, she would have been hurting the company by not clocking in!"

Everyone began to clap. Denny blushed a little, but he stood and gave a bow.

Jacqueline was smiling and clapping, meeting Jane's eyes. They both nodded. Jane would never make assumptions about dishwashers again.

Before Jacqueline could talk, Marcy jumped in. "Denny, thank you. That was great insight, and you helped me to look at this differently." She looked to Jacqueline for permission to continue and got a nod. "And now that I think of it, those managers in previous places were always so worried about numbers tallied on things like payroll that they never looked at the bigger picture. There are ways to be fiscally responsible while also delivering a great experience. I love this!"

"I do too," said Jacqueline. "It is why I will never leave this place unless they kick me out!" Everyone got a chuckle. That wasn't going to happen anytime soon.

For the next couple of hours, the group heard other examples of how the principles had played out, both successfully and unsuccessfully. The latter was amusing to listen to. Jane believed that you learned more from mistakes anyway, and this group was getting into it.

As the group took a break, Jacqueline came over to Jane.

"Well, you might have guessed that I read your book." Jane smiled and nodded.

"But you didn't say anything last night!"

"Well, here's the funny thing. After I got home last night, I looked you up. I saw your book, downloaded it, and read almost all of it."

"Thank you! That is so fun to hear. I was going to go upstairs during the break and bring you a copy. The way you speak and train reminds me of my 'tell me more' strategy. I am really enjoying myself."

"I think that's what made me keep reading as well. I do some of the things you talk about instinctively. The way you talk about them, and the psychological impact, really resonated with me. But to be selfish, I would still love a copy. Autographed, of course."

"Deal!"

"You are certainly welcome to stay for lunch, and the rest of the day as well if you like, but please don't feel obligated. I'm sure you have a lot to do."

"Jacqueline, I didn't know what to expect today, so I didn't know how long I'd stay. If you don't mind, I would love to stay through the day. I am learning so much and want to see what comes next. I'm here to speak at a sales conference on Friday, but today there is nothing urgent. And this is certainly worth my time." Jane didn't want to be a burden on the day, or Jacqueline, but she felt like her brain was on fire with so many ideas.

"We love having you," Jacqueline said while she waved her hands back to the table being set in another part of the restaurant, along with eight wine glasses per place setting. "Enjoy this short break and be ready for a tough lunch!"

"Hm. I think I can handle it."

Chapter 3

LET THEM DRINK WINE!

Jane took a couple of minutes during the break to look over her notes. She was beginning to get some ideas on how to use these principles with some of her clients. She needed a trendy acronym, though — something that would stick in peoples' minds.

When everyone came back from their break, they started to go right to the table set for lunch, but Jacqueline directed them back to their seats.

She set her notebook aside as a woman with deep dark, long hair, and a smart pantsuit joined Jacqueline. She had a strange silver medallion around her neck that, upon closer inspection, Jane thought to be a small shallow cup.

"Team, I want to introduce you to Olivia. Olivia is the Sommelier for the hotel, its restaurants, and of course, at Fred's. Olivia is much more than just our Sommelier, however. She has achieved the title of Master Sommelier. There are only 256 in the world, and of those only, 49 are women."[6]

Olivia nodded appreciatively at the introduction. Jane was impressed, and she could see that her fellow students were as well.

"Let's run around the room quickly so you can give Olivia your name and your position."

The introductions took just a few minutes, and everyone laughed when Jane introduced herself as the new barback. Thankfully, Thomas had explained that to her at the break. Olivia smiled as well. Jacqueline had obviously updated her on why Jane was there.

Once introductions were complete, Jacqueline continued.

"We are fortunate to have her, but you won't often see her in the restaurant. Her job is to make sure each of you, even you Denny," she said, acknowledging him with a nod, "are knowledgeable and passionate about the exquisite wines we serve."

Denny looked a little nervous but still smiled at the attention.

"And with that, I am going to hand things over to Oliva." Jacqueline took a seat at the table with the rest of the students.

"Hello everyone," Olivia said, and the room responded in kind. "Before we move on to lunch and the wine pairings, I want to talk to you about why I became a sommelier. I grew up in Galway, Ireland. My parents owned a pub there, and I worked for them my whole life. As many of you may have done in your career in hospitality, I did everything from tending bar to cooking, and even cleaning the toilets, when needed."

People nodded in understanding.

"One day we had a customer from the States, on holiday. Her family owned a vineyard in Washington State, and we got talking about the challenges and benefits of working for and with family. We had a great time complaining about our parents!"

Olivia's smile was grand. Jane liked her immediately.

"Katherine gave me an open invitation to come to visit, and about a year later, I took her up on it. When I arrived, I was drawn instantly into the beauty of the vineyard. High on a hill overlooking the Yakima River and surrounded by miles and miles of vines with grapes just ready for harvest, it seemed like something out of a fairy tale."[7]

Jane understood that. She loved touring the wineries throughout Washington state. She wanted to know which one Olivia's friend owned, so she could be sure to make a visit.

"When we sat down to the wine tasting, my life changed. I learned about varietals, aging, fermentation, and blends. I saw the beauty of the colors in a glass, experienced aromas that shocked me, and began to understand how you could find tastes like brick dust or tobacco in a glass of red wine."

Everyone in the room seemed enthralled in the picture she was painting.

"Later, we toured the entire facility, and I spoke with the winemakers. I couldn't stop asking them questions. Finally, Katherine's father, the head winemaker, threw up his hands laughing and said, 'Olivia, the only way I can teach you everything you want to know is to make you an apprentice.'

"And so, I did! I stayed for two years, learning everything I could about making wine. I feel like it runs in my veins now alongside my blood." Jane was amazed. What an adventure!

"I could have stayed there forever, and I was certainly welcome to, but I knew I had to come home. My parents were getting ready to retire and had always planned to leave the pub to me. I wasn't sure that was what I still wanted, but I couldn't let them down.

While in the United States, I became a sommelier, and while I was proud of the certification, I had only done it to learn more about wine. Everything to me was another education waiting to be gobbled up. I was always hungry for more."

Jane nodded as she thought about how she too craved knowledge as much as air to breathe.

"But when I returned to the pub, it wasn't enough for me anymore. I missed the wine and knew that our pub wasn't the place to introduce a premium wine selection. I sat down with my parents to discuss my future, and they surprised me by being fully supportive. They sold the pub to one of my cousins, and I went off to travel the world to find more wine."

It is amazing to think about the journeys that people take, Jane thought. She was impressed by Olivia's passion and courage.

"I spent many years in some of the world's finest restaurants and learned about how wine should marry the flavors of food, dove into the changing landscape of corks from actual cork to plastic to screw top, and even found value from wine in a box." Jane smiled at the way Olivia's memories seemed to play out on her face.

"My most memorable lesson was a class I took with an airline sommelier on how altitude affects taste, which included a wine tasting at 10,000, 20,000, and 30,000 feet. Before I knew it, I was on the path to testing as a Master Sommelier."

Jane knew that process was tough, and her respect for Olivia grew considerably. She didn't seek the title for professional gain; she sought it for the love of wine.

"I have been with The Prenton Hotel for six years, and it has been the most challenging and satisfying point in my career. Today I want to share my expectations with you."

That got everyone's attention again. Olivia's story was compelling enough on its own, but the fact that she had expectations of the staff reignited the seriousness of this training and the level of professionalism expected from everyone in the hotel.

"Now, if you would come with me, I'd like to introduce you to my family," Olivia said with a bright smile. Everyone stood up, looking a little confused.

Until that is, Olivia took them to the wine cellar.

Although the bar had one beautiful wall highlighting bottles of wine, Jane now realized that the wall wasn't just for show. It was the entryway to a subterranean showcase.

Olivia waited until everyone was in the entryway and the glass door closed before opening a second, well-aged wooden door that led down a flight of steps. At the bottom, Jane found herself in a cellar of stellar proportions. Racks and racks of wine, some dusty, some spotless, lined the walls and made aisles through the entire room. Other than some of the wine rooms at commercial vineyards, Jane had never seen so much wine in one place.

After giving everyone a minute to look around, eyes wide and some mouths open in awe, she began to speak again.

"I consider these wines to be my family. Each one is unique, lovely, and precious. Each one has a talent. One may unlock the richness of a perfectly cooked filet. One has the perfect balance of bubbles and sweetness to pair with toasted walnuts and fresh figs, and others pair perfectly with a breakup." Olivia smiled at the last, and when her statement caught up to everyone, there was soft laughter.

"Seriously though, I want you to understand how much care I have put into selecting our wines and that each guest should feel like we have chosen, recommended and served them something that we would be proud to call family."

Jane was intrigued by that concept. It made it so personal. And a little daunting.

As she looked around, she could tell others felt the same way. She saw that Olivia noticed as well.

"So, you might feel a little overwhelmed by all I've said," she said, laughing. Everyone nodded.

"I am not surprised. I promise I haven't been sampling my product already this morning." Now the laughter was a bit more relaxed, and Olivia's smile helped to change the tone.

"OK, let's have some fun. Who here has drunk wine?" Everyone raised a hand.

"Who likes wine?" Every hand rose, although some people looked a little sheepish, including Marcy.

"Marcy, you seem to be nervous to tell me something. Fess up."

Marcy laughed and shrugged. "You caught me. I will drink wine, but it isn't my favorite. I prefer beer."

"Thank you for sharing that Marcy. You probably aren't alone in this room, but you are the bravest." Olivia let a fake cranky look pass over the rest of the group, and people relaxed even more.

"I don't expect any of you to become wine fanatics at all. You can all pass by the wine pairings at lunch if you'd like." Everyone assured her that they certainly would *not* pass up the wine. The laughter then showed that the team was back to comfort and ease.

"But what I do want you to understand is this: When someone orders a glass or a bottle of wine, *they are* fanatics. Maybe they are only passionate for that one meal or that one evening, but they are ordering wine for a reason. And that means that we have a responsibility to give them an amazing wine experience."

That made sense to Jane and the rest of the team nodded along with her. If they want wine, let them drink wine! And honor the wine in that interaction.

"We have over 5,000 bottles of wine here, from more than 350 vintners and more than 20 countries." Jane was in awe. "That comes down to about 1,200 options, and you'll be tested on your knowledge of every one."

Heads whipped toward her, fear in the eyes of everyone, including Jane!

Olivia let that settle until she couldn't hold back the laughter anymore.

"Don't look so afraid. I am going to show you how." That statement didn't allay any fears.

"I don't expect you to know all of these," she said as she gestured to the room. "But I do expect you to know how to give people options.

Often servers have a couple of wines that they become comfortable with, like those that we'll serve with lunch today and those that we taste with the staff when we add them to the cellar. But that doesn't allow our customers to browse the whole collection. And we must beware of us deciding what the customer wants."

Heads nodded in agreement.

"We do, of course, have a wine list. Most people go only as far as the first few pages, or they skip directly to a varietal they like. Some scan for a price point and guess. But those are not the experiences we want people to have with our wines."

Jane nodded as did others. She did that herself. She didn't often go to places with sommeliers, and if she did, they often intimated her just as much as an extensive wine list. She preferred others to make the wine choices in those situations.

"To that end, I developed something for the hotel that allows you to have access to every wine we have available and to give customers a truly unique experience."

Jane found herself leaning forward, eager for whatever this was. She found Thomas leaning in as well. They looked at each other and smiled.

"Would you like to know what it is that will give each of you knowledge on these 1,200 options?" She said with a wink, as everyone practically yelled their agreement.

Jacqueline began passing around small tablets, with a strap on the back to allow your hand to slide in and hold the device snugly in the palm. At that moment a monitor lit up on a wall, mirroring what they each saw on their tablet.

"Jacqueline and your department managers will be showing other ways you will work with these throughout the day, but right now you are all keyed up to your wine page. Who wants to be my volunteer?"

Everyone stuck up a hand, and Olivia called on James, a server who had been somewhat silent through the morning.

"James, do you have a type of wine you like?"

"Hm. Good question. I like red wine!" He made this statement emphatically and with a giant boyish smile. Everyone laughed, including Olivia.

"Perfect James! Now everyone, go to the filter button and pick red please." Jane was intrigued to see that you could choose any combination of red, white, rose, sparkling and dessert. After the filter, Jane saw the options reduced from more than 1,200 to a little more than 650.

Holy Smokes! Jane thought. *How can you get through that many options?*

"What kinds of red wines do you like, James?"

"I like full body wines. I don't like soft ones. I think red wine should be big and powerful."

Olivia nodded and instructed everyone to filter for the terms full, big, and powerful. 'Powerful' wasn't an option in the drop-down menu, but Olivia showed them where to type it in. The number of potential wines changed to about 300.

"You see, not everyone will use all of the same terms. But I want to make sure that we can use the customer's words as much as possible. The app uses artificial intelligence to use like-words to make connections, and we update the app weekly to make sure it is adapting.

What else, James? Do you like any particular varietals like Cabernet or Merlot?"

"I tend to drink Cabs because they fit those criteria, but I have been surprised by others as well. So, I guess I'm open."

Olivia had them filter for both Cabernet and a button that said 'open.'

"James just gave us a wonderful example. In my experience, many people are open to other things but don't always know how to look for or ask for something out of their comfort zone. So, it would be easy to recommend a Cabernet or Cab varietal. He would be comfortable with that." Everyone nodded, and Jane anticipated what Olivia would say next.

"But I don't want to give James what he expects. I want to give him options that he could explore if he wanted to. So, if he is open to other varietals, I want to be able to filter for that. Does that make sense to everyone?"

Everyone was practically bouncing on their toes now, fully invested, and excited to see where this would lead. The "open" filter brought them to just over 100 options.

"A couple more questions, James. First, are there any countries that you are particularly fond of for their wine?"

"Hm. I love French wines, some from Napa in the United States, and I've had some great ones from South Africa. But I am open in this area too."

That led to more filtering for France, US/Napa and then 'open" which Jane thought would still leave them with the same number of options for when they picked France and US/Napa, but to her surprise, the list went down to just under 50.

"Jane, I see you are confused. Why?"

"Well, I assumed the 'open' filter would still keep it open to all of the wines from the last filter. Why even filter for France and Napa and South Africa if he is open? Shouldn't that still give you the same number of choices?"

But as the question came out, Jane realized she might know the answer.

"I think you might just have figured it out," said Olivia. "James did give us three countries and areas, and the app filters the remaining wines for similar characteristics. It's not an exact science, but it does help narrow the field. The remaining wines from the 'open' filter will have similar profiles to what he has enjoyed."

Everyone nodded agreement.

"Now, for the last question, James. What price points are you looking for with your meal tonight, monsieur?" Olivia asked the last question in an outrageous French accent, making everyone smile.

"I usually buy in the 20 to30-pound range for a nice evening out." Everyone added the last filter, leaving them with a selection of 23 wines, all complete with descriptions, ratings, and food pairing suggestions that matched the restaurant offerings.

This is incredible! Jane thought. James agreed by his giant smile and response of "Amazeballs!"[8]

"You'll be able to sync this data with a tablet at the table so the guests can review and even play with the selection criteria. What we find is that people will, more often than not, choose a wine they have never had before."

This is Olivia's version of 'tell me more,' Jane thought. *And it takes the intimidation factor down several notches.*

"And something else. Who can tell me what our third core expectation is?" Everyone's hands went up, including Jane's. She certainly felt like a part of this team.

When Olivia called on Denny, he said, "Be creative in how we WOW our customers, and make sure you WOW this hotel that signs our paycheck by making them money!"

Everyone got a chuckle out of that, including Olivia and Jacqueline. "Well, I can't say I've heard it put quite that way before," said Olivia, "but I couldn't agree more. So, I think you will enjoy this last point."

She leaned in, seeming to gather everyone into her as if ready to impart a great secret. "And since we began using these tablets, the average price of wine sold has gone up by over 7 percent. I'd say that we created a definite WOW with the company."

Heads nodded, and everyone could see the value in that type of financial outcome. Jane was even more pleased that she was lucky enough to be a part of this training.

"So, as you can see, I take our three core expectations very seriously, and I want our patrons to feel a part of their journey with us, whether they are ordering a cocktail, a steak, an incredible glass of wine, or simply enjoying the beauty of our hotel. They should be at the core of everything we do."

Jane certainly could see that, and her mind was running wild at how much the core expectations of The Prenton Hotel fell in line with her *Tell Me More* strategy. By engaging the customer in questions, in many ways, the customer plays a part in ensuring a fantastic experience.

As Jacqueline gathered everyone to return upstairs for lunch, Olivia fell in beside Jane. "I'm so glad you decided to join us today, Jane. Jacqueline gave me a heads up on what you're doing here. What do you think so far?"

"Olivia, this has been some of the best education I have ever had, and I teach this stuff for a living!" Both women smiled.

"I am so glad to hear that," Olivia said, smiling. "This place is extraordinary. My family gave me all kinds of grief for moving to Northern Ireland, but when the position came up, I had to take a chance on it."

"I can see why The Prenton does so well," said Jane. "This level of attention to detail and customer service is something really special. And it shows, in everything I have seen so far."

"Well, then hold on to your seat, Jane. Lunch is served."

Chapter 4

LUNCH IS SERVED

Lunch was an unforgettable experience, with descriptions by Chef Marcos on every course, alongside Olivia's introduction of each wine. It was an education that Jane would have never imagined having outside of culinary school.

The attention to detail on each dish was exquisite, and Jane realized she had never given much thought to the importance of the garnish. Most of the world was undoubtedly past an orange wedge and a sprig of curly parsley on the side of a plate, but creating a specific garnish for a dish was like adding the finishing touches to a Picasso.

A radish carved into a rose, an edible flower, even painting a plate with pureed beets created not only a visually stimulating picture but also showed a higher level of intent and attention to the customer. Steps like this added cost, and they took vast amounts of additional time, but they were part of an overall and intentional strategy.

Jane made a mental note to pay more attention to details like that around her. What was she taking for granted when she should be valuing the heightened experience?

Chef Marcos continued. "Now that you have all sampled our most popular dishes, there are some things I need you to know that I expect of you." The group was getting used to this kind of talk, but even Jane wondered *what now*?

"I know Olivia shared her expectations with you to help our customers find a wine that they love." Everyone nodded.

"The same should be said for the food they choose. Individual tastes and desires need to be our primary objective. Just as Olivia wants them to find a wine that they love, so too do I want them to find food that they love."

This made sense to Jane and the others in the room. But Jane wondered about this statement. The wine was one thing. It could be intimidating for someone to pick a wine with which they weren't familiar. But how many people would be intimidated by choosing steak over fish?

As Chef Marcos continued, however, she began to understand.

"Let me give you an example of what I mean. I think role-play does it best. Who wants to be my volunteer?" Nervous glances abounded, but Denny stood up. Jane had a feeling Denny wouldn't be a dishwasher for long.

"Excellent Denny. Now I will be the customer, and you will be the server," Chef Marcos said as he sat down. "I want you to ask me what I want for dinner, and we'll see where it goes from there."

Looking a little apprehensive while trying to appear confident, Denny forged forward.

"Welcome to Fred's, sir. What may I get you for dinner?" Denny asked with enthusiasm.

"Hm. I am not sure. What do you recommend?"

"Ah ... the Steak Tartar is amazing."

"I'm vegan."

"Well then, the Primavera Pasta is lovely."

Denny smiled, and so did the rest of the room, now that everyone had an idea of what was coming next.

"I am gluten intolerant," said Chef Marcos.

Denny smiled and said, "Then I recommend a lovely selection of water!"

Everyone smiled and laughed, including Chef Marcos as he indicated for Denny to take a seat. Denny took a little bow. He knew he had not succeeded in his task, but he seemed content.

"As you can see, I set out to purposefully torture Denny. But there is a lesson to be learned here. Denny, what do you think that is?"

"I wanted to give you an answer. You asked what I recommended, and since we had two of those delicious dishes today at lunch, I was eager to share my favorites. But what I failed to do was ask you questions. If I had done that, I could have narrowed down your limitations."

"Spot on, Denny. We are often so eager to give answers or share things that we like that it is easy to fall into our own experiences and miss that of the customer. We must be aware of times we might unwittingly be influencing the customer with our tastes, rather than helping them to explore what they want." Jane pondered that a moment, as did the rest.

"I'm not saying that you can't make recommendations," Chef Marcos went on. "But even when a customer asks us what we recommend, we must be wary that we don't make decisions for or assumptions about the customer."

Olivia jumped in for a moment, and Jane could see that they played this part off each other often. It was the moment she realized that the entire company knew what the people in different roles were doing, and cared. They worked this training together to make sure the whole staff continued to work together to achieve the mission.

"Remember when I told you that servers would often recommend a wine that *they* have enjoyed and are comfortable with?" Everyone nodded to Olivia's question, and the light bulbs were beginning to go off.

"You now see that the choice of wine should *never* be about *our* tastes. It should only be about the tastes of our customer. That is why the wine app is so valuable."

Chef Marcos picked right up. Jane loved the flow between the two of them; it was like a well-rehearsed play.

"And although we don't use an app for dinner choices," Chef Marcos continued, "We can use the same strategy through the questions that we ask to achieve the same result." People nodded, and many now leaned physically into the discussion.

"Let's try it again. Denny, will you do the honors again, but this time as the customer, and using the exact same answers I gave you to my questions?"

Denny nodded, stuffed his napkin in the neck of his shirt, and asked in a stuffy tone, "My good man, what do you recommend for dinner tonight?"

Chef Marcos, who moved back to stand in front of Denny said, "Sir, we have a lovely selection of entrees tonight. Let me ask you a few questions to narrow down my recommendations. Do you feel like fish, meat or a vegetarian option tonight?"

"I am a vegan."

"Excellent sir. Do you prefer a meal with starch or pasta?"

"I am gluten intolerant."

"No problem, sir. We have three entrée choices for you that meet your dietary needs exactly. Additionally, we have several starter selections that could be combined to serve as a very fulfilling dinner. Many of our entrees can be made both vegan and gluten-free. You will find a notation by each dish on what can be accommodated to specific dietary needs. Let me describe a few for you and show you where to find them on the menu."

Everyone was nodding now. It still came down to questions. Ask the right ones, in the right way, at the right time, and you will deliver on an experience crafted for an individual customer.

The rest of the day was a blur for Jane. She thoroughly enjoyed the afternoon session with William, the Director of Mixology, and Ken. They even showed her and Thomas how to make the cocktail Ken made Jane the night before. When the entire team came together at the end of the day to recap before dinner prep, Jane felt exhausted. Her mind, however, was racing with ideas. Jacqueline brought them all back to seriousness.

 It still came down to questions. Ask the right ones, in the right way, at the right time, and you will deliver on an experience crafted for an individual customer.

"You all did a great job today, and I am confident that each of you will make a fantastic addition to our team." Everyone was smiling, feeling her confidence, including Jane.

"We expect a lot of you because our customers expect a lot out of us. When you come in each day, leave the problems in your life behind. You can escape those issues for a time while giving someone else a memorable experience. And you will find that your life-view will improve as well when you are putting others first daily."

Jane understood that. It was a kind of a glass-half-full view to keep a half-full, or more, glass of positivity.

"We also have a zero tolerance for gossip or complaining." Everyone perked up at this and Jane was a bit surprised that it came out at the end of the day.

"Let me explain why we have this policy, and why I am telling you now at the end of the day." She smiled at Jane knowingly. She must have read her mind or her facial expression.

"We spent the entire day showing you how we operate as one team to achieve our core expectations. 'The customer, and their experience, *always* comes first. No one person or one position is more important than creating and maintaining an excellent customer experience.

And each day you will be expected to find ways to deliver on our first promise, while also building the financial success of the company.' We can't do any of those things if we don't operate as one team dedicated to those expectations."

People nodded, but Jacqueline and Jane could see they didn't all get it. Gossip tended to be a mainstay in any work environment, and Jane had yet to rid a company of people complaining about co-workers and managers. But she could see the purpose of making this attempt.

"If any of you have an issue with anyone else in the company, we want it resolved. Try first to resolve it on your own, and if that doesn't work, follow the chain of command in your department. No one's bad behavior, even yours," Jacqueline said, pointing at Jane with a snarl, drawing a laugh, "will be allowed to affect our core expectations. We are all adults. We will operate like adults. We will resolve conflict like adults."

Jacqueline looked around and watched as people nodded, a little nervously.

"Complaining about any work issue proves that something is not right. It might be with a person or a process, or even a customer, but if there is a problem, and we don't solve it, everything we are trying to achieve falls apart." That made sense to everyone, but it was clear that no one believed it was possible. After all, people complained in every work situation. Could you really eradicate it?

Jacqueline could see the disbelief, and it was clear that she had seen the same doubt many times over.

"Chef Marcos, will you help me with an example?" He stepped right up, nodding. "Will you share with the group the conflict we had when I first started?"

This made Jane perk up, as well as those around her. But it was clear that the question didn't seem to upset Chef Marcos at all.

"Absolutely," he said. "When Jacqueline first started, I was concerned about how she wanted to include every member of my kitchen staff in the training. I had never put a busser or a dishwasher through any training like this. I thought it was a waste of time and money." Everyone looked at Denny, who smiled and raised his hands in a gesture of 'it's not my fault,' making Chef Marcos laugh.

"Exactly, Denny! I stewed on it for a few weeks, before I went to Sandra, the General Manager. Although I hadn't said anything to anyone else, by the time I got to Sandra's office, I was pretty hot about it. I was watching my payroll go up, which is an important measurement for any kitchen." Everyone nodded, and Jane looked immediately to Marcy, who had brought that up as a topic earlier in the day, and saw her smiling. She could already anticipate the ending of this story.

"Sandra asked me if I had gone to Jacqueline about my concerns, and I had to admit that I had not. I sheepishly walked out of her office and found Jacqueline. We sat down to talk, and I was surprised to find that we talked nonstop for almost an hour. I asked her why she wanted to do this, what she expected to gain, and if she knew what it cost me in terms of payroll."

Jacqueline smiled and nodded and gestured for him to continue.

"Then, seeming to ignore my questions, she began asking me questions about what I needed in my team. She asked about my most pressing needs, my biggest headaches, and my greatest challenges. It wasn't long before I realized that her strategy would help me build and keep a productive and profitable kitchen. I just had to trust in, and invest in, training and people development."

Jacqueline jumped in then. "Before Chef Marcos takes this all on his shoulders, what he isn't saying is how I failed him initially." People were really getting into this. "I had my plan. I had been successful in this strategy elsewhere with a smaller hotel, and I wanted to prove myself quickly. Sandra had approved my plan, so I came in ready to make change happen fast."

"But what I failed to do was get the buy-in from my colleagues before I began. I didn't take the time to ask those initial questions to learn about their pain points as well as their vision for their department. Even though I knew what I was doing was going to have great benefit to the company, it had no benefit to anyone else unless I verified that we were all looking for the same results."

Jane saw that same issue with so many of the companies with which she worked. Everyone was trying to achieve their own goals as fast and furious as possible, always afraid deep down that if they stopped long enough to get buy-in that they not only might get push-back, they might also fail to deliver results.

But how do you prove results to people who don't believe in the first place?

"So," Jacqueline continued, "I slowed down, took stock and started again. I sat down with each department manager to ask them the right questions, the right way, and explained not only my strategy and how it had been successful before on a smaller scale, but how I wanted to find ways to incorporate them in the training process." With this last statement, she indicated to all the department managers that were in the room, including Sandra, who had arrived when Jane wasn't looking.

"And," Chef Marcos continued, "if I had only complained about Jacqueline to my colleagues, or kept my frustrations to myself, I would have done the entire company a disservice. She was right.

I was wrong. But the only thing that mattered is that together we could, and would, make this place something unique."

"None of us is perfect," said Sandra, finally stepping up. "So, each one of you in this room will forget about the no-gossip, no-complain policy at least a few times. That's why I expect each of you to help each other. If one of you has an issue and is complaining around the water cooler, we have a safe way of engaging the topic. Say, 'I understand. Let's find the solution together.'"

 I expect each of you to help each other. If one of you has an issue and is complaining around the water cooler, we have a safe way of engaging the topic. Say, "I understand. Let's find the solution together."

Jane nodded as did others. That made sense. Give a sort of safe word or phrase to allow you to call someone out on their words without making it a big deal, and at the same time remind them that you are all in it together.

"And," Sandra continued, "this strategy has allowed us to enjoy a significant reduction in turnover and a significant increase in internal promotions. People that accept this mission find it a satisfying place to work." Jane could see the smiles and nods of everyone in the room, including her fellow new employees who were beginning to understand what a unique place they had just signed on with.

As the group broke up, each person going to their team to help prep for dinner service, Sandra and Jacqueline came up to Jane. Olivia, Chef Marcos, and the other department managers all waved goodbye, along with Jane's fellow classmates.

"Well, what do you think of our little family here?" Sandra said with a smile as she sat down next to Jane at the chair James had just left.

Jane tilted her head, nodded, and smiled. "I have learned more today than I have in the last 10 years of my career. You have something special here, and I am so honored to have been a part of it."

Sandra smiled, beaming almost as a parent over a compliment to their child. "Thank you so much for saying so, Jane." At that moment Jacqueline walked up, free of her last-minute training responsibilities.

"Seriously," Jane continued. "You are doing something unique here. You have also made me think about how sometimes experiences polarize us." Both women looked a little confused by the statement.

"When someone has an awful customer experience, they remember it and are often vocal about it. And they can often recount that experience for many years." Sandra and Jacqueline nodded in understanding.

"And when someone has a great experience, they are elated about it, but usually only for a short while." Everyone nodded again.

"You are working here to create consistently overwhelmingly positive experiences. But it makes me wonder if we can become numb to experiences that are always good."

Both women looked confused again. Jane laughed.

"I apologize. My brain often works faster than my ability to communicate." Sandra and Jacqueline encouraged her to go on.

"You make this all look and feel seamless. You have empowered your team to be great, all the time. Do you ever worry that people will expect higher levels of excellence from you?"

Sandra laughed, and Jacqueline smiled. "That is a great question, Jane. It is the reason the training you participated in here is only the first step of many." Jane was hoping, and anticipating, that there might be more.

"We believe that on-going training is not only worth the investment, but that it is the most important investment we make in our company."

"As you know," she continued, "turnover is the greatest challenge we face in the hospitality industry. Front line staff turnover, like food and beverage workers, front desk and housekeeping staff can be as high as 110 percent, and management positions turnover about 20 to 30 percent." Jane nodded, but she was a bit shocked by the numbers.

"The cost of those turnovers, however," Sandra continued, "is something that many businesses just look at as the cost of doing business." Jane nodded again, as did Jacqueline.

"Just in number alone, the cost is staggering. It costs us at least $2,000 to $5,000 per front line position, and at least $10,000 to $15,000 per management position."[9]

Jane wasn't surprised; she had seen similar numbers in other companies.

"But more than the financial cost, we were not satisfied with the human cost." Sandra smiled at Jane's puzzled look.

"We believe that we hire the best people to be a part of the best team, to provide the best service, for the life of the company." Jane nodded again, knowing she saw that in action today.

"And when someone leaves us, whether their choice or ours, we have failed them."

"OK, I have been with you through that all," Jane said, "up until that last part. You can't retain everyone. It's not even possible!"

Jacqueline laughed and said, "Jane, just because it isn't probable, doesn't mean it isn't possible."

Jane had to laugh then, knowing she was caught. It was a line from own her book talking about creating a workplace so healthy and productive that people couldn't wait to get to work each day and be a part of it.

"Using my own words against me, I see," Jane said, laughing along with Jacqueline and Sandra. "I suppose I know what you mean now. Just because you might not be able to save them all doesn't mean you shouldn't try."

They nodded their agreement, and Sandra took up the dialogue once again.

"Jane, there are many different scenarios here. First, if we hire the *wrong* person and they don't work out, we must review where we went wrong in the hiring process. Next, if we hire the *right* person and they don't work out, we must review where we failed them in the training and development phase. And finally, if we hired the *right* person but they leave for any reason other than they have to move, we have to review what we could have done to keep them. Does that make sense?"

"Yes, it does. I always say that you have to have the right person, in the right position, doing the right things. If you have the right person, but they are in the wrong position or doing the wrong things, it is your responsibility to change that. I also say that if you have the wrong person, however, then none of the rest matters. But now I realize that I am missing the question about why you hired the wrong person in the first place."

"That is exactly it," Sandra said. "We don't beat ourselves up over losses, but we do learn from them. And because of this attention, we have reduced our turnover from those averages I shared with you to about 50 percent for front line staff and around 10 percent for management positions. Considering how many people we employ, that is staggering."

Jacqueline jumped in then. "But we won't quit until we reach zero percent turnover!" And with that statement, each of them laughed. Jane couldn't help but remember her *Home Away* clients on their mission to reach and maintain 100 percent occupancy in their assisted living facilities. One hundred percent occupancy might not be probable, but it was possible.

"But there is one more element you haven't seen yet," added Jacqueline. "We take ongoing training very seriously here. You have seen just one of our elements in motion here today. There are a few others that I can introduce you to on Wednesday if you are interested."

"Are you kidding me?" Jane asked. "Of course, I want to know!"

Right then, Sandra stood and said, "Well, I'll leave you two to work out the rest of the details. I need to get this restaurant ready to open." Sandra smiled, stood, and headed back to the team.

"Jacqueline, this was an amazing day. I can't imagine how much more you have up your sleeve, but I am excited to see it. Where should I be, and when?"

"Meet me at my office on the fourth floor around 1:45 p.m. on Wednesday. We'll see what you think of our continuing education program."

Jane and Jacqueline shared a hug, said goodbye, and Jane took a moment to look around as the dining room came alive. Her class, alongside their tenured colleagues, was prepping for dinner, and the quiet of the day earlier was now replaced by a lovely hum.

Jane had been in drama in high school and college and realized that Jacqueline had been right. This room had been like an empty stage and auditorium before anyone arrived that morning. But now it reminded her of the last few moments before a production. Behind the curtain, actors, stagehands, musicians, and directors were brimming with nervous excitement, peeking circumspectly to see how the seats were filling. All of them ready to perform at their best individually, and as a cast.

As she walked out smiling, she felt like she had just been allowed an all-access backstage pass.

Chapter 5

THE RIGHT BLEND

When Jane got to her room, she was exhausted. Between the last vestiges of jet lag and an entire day of being a pupil, she fell happily on to her bed to put her feet up for a bit. She thought she would catch a quick nap before going to grab some dinner, but the thoughts running through her head kept her from dozing.

She kept thinking about how all of the concepts discussed today applied to so many of the businesses with which she worked. She finally got up from the bed and started looking through her notes.

Jane laughed when she saw how many notes she had taken on the wines they had with lunch. She had so much fun learning how Olivia and Chef Marcos determined how each one paired and complimented the menu. It was inspiring. It was like food and wine worked together in harmony, one blended into the other.

Blend. Wait.

There was something there. Jane furiously began to scribble, write, cross out, and write again. About 10-minutes later, on a blank piece of paper, Jane had the answer:

B – Be Immediately and Fully Present

L – Listen with Your Ears AND Your Eyes

E – Ensure That You Have Asked All the Right Questions

N – Never Let Your Customer Feel like a Number

D – Deliver an Exceptional Customer Experience
(Being Mindful of Financial Return)

Let's see how this matches my first experience at Fred's, Jane thought. She then jotted a note to see how it played out.

B – Be Immediately and Fully Present

Jane hardly had time to settle in her seat before Ken had reached her. She had been acknowledged immediately upon entering the restaurant, and that alone made her pause.

Because she always sat at the bar to eat dinner while traveling, she was, sadly, used to having the bartender ignore her for the first few moments. Or, if not ignored, immediately pressed by the question, "What can I get you to drink?" Although not an inappropriate question, it always felt sterile.

Even more often, the bartender was on his or her phone, and Jane felt she was intruding on their screen time. Ken, on the other hand, made her feel that her experience was the only reason he came into work that day.

L – Listen with Your Ears AND Your Eyes

Ken's questions ensured that he was trying to find the right fit for her. Even more surprising was how quickly he recognized her angst at the group of people that entered, making her feel guilty for taking his time. He had been watching her closely and knew what had caused her concern. He alleviated that concern immediately and was able to help her reengage with her experience.

E – Ensure That You Have Asked All the Right Questions

Even with all of the questions he asked her, Ken still gave Jane the power of choice. There were a lot of questions, but they didn't take up much time at all. And through the questions, Jane was not only satisfied with her decision, but also felt valued in the process.

N – Never Let Your Customer Feel Like a Number

Now that Jane thought about it, she realized that although it felt like Ken was always watching only her for what she needed next, he was also doing that with every other person at the bar.

She had to laugh at herself. Until this minute, she thought it was all about her. The fact that he also juggled 15 or 20 other customers at the bar, while also overseeing the bar needs of the servers, was a testament to Ken and The Prenton team. Every single person probably felt like they were the only one receiving such personalized attention.

D – Deliver an Exceptional Customer Experience (While Being Mindful of Financial Return)

There was no doubt in Jane's mind that her experience encouraged her to stay longer and want to return. Those two things alone would always generate a financial return for a company. But if you multiply that by all the people committed to the company mission, this had to be one of the most profitable hotels around.

She set down her pen. That was it. She felt like she had a concept that would be fun to work with and share, and it was applicable in any industry.

From the moment she first walked into Fred's the night before, she could see that the restaurant delivered on all of those promises. She began to think about the companies she worked with, including the upcoming group of spa professionals. What was true for a fantastic cocktail experience was just as true for a great spa experience. After all, when you show up for your massage or facial, you expect to feel pampered.

No longer able to contemplate a nap, Jane began to write. The words flowed easily, and she could see her second book beginning to form. Before she knew it, however, she was hungry and headed out of the hotel in search of dinner.

As she walked, her mind continued to process all that she had learned. It made her wonder about experiences of all kinds and reminded her of the question she had posed to Sandra and Jacqueline earlier. Could you become numb to great experiences? If one company consistently delivered on those promises, would it begin to lose its initial luster? Or could you become more aware of the joy in that consistent experience?

Jane thought about her local pharmacy, a chain pharmacy close to her house, where she went a couple of times every week for one thing or another. They had a surprisingly vast supply of vital things like office supplies, kitchen items, and, of course, an abundance of her downfall — Red Vines.

She realized she never had a bad experience there. Ever. The team was consistently good. She was always greeted when she entered. If she had a problem, it was quickly fixed with no drama. If they were out of something she wanted, they would order it. She felt that they valued the business of everyone that walked in the door. So why didn't she pay more attention to how this consistently excellent service was a sign of greatness?[10]

Jane turned a corner, and one pub seemed to call her name from the street. Smiling people walked out, and there were sounds of laughing and the buzz of joyful conversation every time the door opened.

Once inside, Jane found a spot at the end of a shared table in front of a huge roaring fireplace. She was getting used to the decadence of fireplaces in restaurants. After ordering the seafood chowder, she sat back to observe the room.

Business people, families, people on dates, and friends were all happily laughing and chatting. In one corner, two musicians filled the place with great music that added to the charm but was not so loud as to distract from conversations. All in all, it was wonderful. Again, she wished her husband was there with her, but his work kept him from being able to join her on this trip.

"May we share your table?" came a question from two gentlemen. Jane hadn't even noticed the people who shared her table left. She had been fully engrossed in the picturesque scene.

"Absolutely!" Jane responded and shifted down slightly so they could get in without trouble.

"I love your hair!" said the man who first spoke, and his companion nodded in agreement. "It is so fun!"

"Thank you," Jane responded with a smile. "I began to do it a few years ago when I realized there was a perfectly acceptable connection between professionalism and personality. I went with it and never looked back. I do like to change the colors often, though."

"I'm Jack," said the first man. "And this is Stephen." Jane introduced herself and shook their hands. "What brings you to Belfast, Jane?"

"I am speaking at a spa industry conference on Friday and decided to come a few days early to see the city. I've never been to Northern Ireland before."

"Welcome! What is the topic you will be speaking on?" Stephen asked.

"I am here to speak on sales leadership and was invited by the executive director of the association after she read my book, *Tell Me More*. Four thousand people will be captivated by my brilliance!" Jane said, and winked.

"Four thousand people, eh? That sounds a little daunting. You don't get nervous in front of all those people?" Jack asked, seriously.

"Nope. Not at all; I love it. What do you gentlemen do?"

At that moment, Jane received her chowder along with a side of soda bread that was hot, smelled fresh out of the oven and made her mouth water. Considering how much she had eaten at lunch, she was surprised that she was so hungry. Jack and Stephen ordered their pints and motioned her to eat.

"We design shoes," Jack said. "I have a passion for creative and colorful women's shoes, and Stephen here makes men's serious business shoes with nothing creative about them whatsoever." Jane had to laugh when Stephen playfully punched Jack in the arm.

"OK! I fess up," Jack laughed. "Stephen creates incredibly attractive professional men's shoes with surprising details that allow men to let their personality shine through."

Stephen picked up the conversation. "You know how colorful men's socks are now the rage?" Jane nodded, thinking of how her husband laughed and rolled his eyes when she brought him home an outrageous pair of neon green socks decorated with frogs from her last trip to London. He did wear them, though.

"Well, I've taken it a few steps further. I incorporate designs that are sometimes hidden, sometimes in plain view but not always immediately recognizable. It's almost a little personal boycott of the traditional black suit with black dress shoes."

"I love it!" Jane exclaimed. "I have quite a collection of fun and fabulous shoes myself, so I most definitely need to know more about yours." Inside she wondered how many pairs of shoes she would bring home this trip, and what her husband would have to say about that.

"We spotted your style and flair the moment we walked in," Jack said. "I guess we are drawn to our target demographic. Call it guerrilla marketing!" They all laughed at that.

"But seriously, Jane," Jack said. "Stephen and I came here tonight to decide on the next steps with our company, *Stepping Out*. We have a nice solid team, but we are expecting a massive contract soon. If all goes well, our company will need to expand rapidly and exponentially. Now that we know what you do, any advice for a small, close-knit company to manage a rapid expansion while also making sure we continue to provide a great customer experience?"

"If you don't mind us picking your brain, that is," Stephen added. "We are shamelessly asking for free advice." He gave Jack a look that was supposed to be withering.

Jane laughed. "I would be happy to give you some thoughts. Tell me more. What are your biggest concerns right now?"

"Well," Jack said, "we are a boutique company with direct access to our customers. Some shop in our stores, others online, and we've worked hard so that both customers trust our products, the experience and us. We deliver on our promises and work hard to ensure that whether someone buys in-store or online, that they feel they had a great experience as well purchased an incredible pair of shoes. We're afraid we could lose that by expanding too fast and having our product sold through channels where we don't control the sales process."

"Tell me more. What do you do now that makes Stepping Out stand out from the competition?"

Stephen jumped in this time. "I think we'd have to break that down by in-store and online." Jack and Jane both nodded, encouraging him to go on.

"Our stores are quite lovely and unique. We want people to walk in and immediately feel like they are in their walk-in closet. We have turned the retail store model on its head." Jack, who had pulled out a tablet, nodded enthusiastically and turned the tablet around to see the inside of one of their stores.

"Wow!" Jane said. "That truly is something unique. It looks like a walk-in closet! I feel like I am in a closet from an episode of *Lifestyles of the Rich and Fam*ous."

"Yes!" Jack exclaimed. "That is what we were going for — a sense of luxury beyond what you may have. Or, if you do, a place that would make you feel at home. We want it to be inviting and exciting."

"Your store certainly gives a unique visual experience," Jane said. "What else about how you operate in-store ensures that you deliver a great experience?"

"Our staff trains constantly," Stephen continued. "We want them current not only on trends, but also on fitting issues, sales techniques, store displays, and more. We use a Mystery Shopping platform as well. Each one of our stores is shopped at least monthly, and the management team reviews, evaluates and adapts store and company plans based on the results of those sessions."[11]

That certainly appealed to Jane. She made a mental note to learn more how Stepping Out worked.

"We also have highly targeted methods for encouraging repeat sales," said Jack. Jane loved how the two were such a tag team of information.

"We have pre-determined touch points with a specific method for the touch. Phone, text, email, mail and presents," Stephen said with a twinkle in his eye.

"Presents?" Jane asked, clearly intrigued.

"Yes. We have some extremely loyal customers, and also new customers that strike us as becoming raving fans. Any customer who has purchased two or more pairs of shoes within the calendar year receives a small gift each March. It might be leather polish, a shoe horn, shoe bags for travel."

Jane nodded, thinking this clever.

"We have also found it valuable to send out free shoes from our new collections to select customers. The social media posts create a lot of buzz, but we reap the biggest rewards when they wear the shoes out in public on any given day in any situation."

Jane wanted in on this action, and said as much, making them all laugh.

"Seriously though," Jack continued, "even though we love to see them on celebrities on a red carpet or media appearances, we want everyday people to wear them, love them, and cause people to ask where they got them. I can guarantee you this, Jane. If you walked into our store tomorrow, you would buy shoes and have gifts coming. Knowing what you do for a living, we would be putting our shoes on stages all around the world."

Jane had to admit, that would be very fun indeed. Now she was quite confident she would have to make room for more shoes on her way home.

"That sounds well thought out," Jane said. "How do you make the online experience unique?"

"That is the bigger challenge now, isn't it?" Stephen went on. "We have segmented our customers to help this process."

Now Jane was intrigued.

"First, all customers are filtered in our system. First-time customers are handled differently from repeat customers. First-time customers have a certain series of prompts while they are on the site. Special offers, suggestions for ancillary products, and more are designed specifically for a new user," Stephen said.

That made sense to Jane. She knew of other retailers who did similar things.

"But the messages we send aren't just the usual 'need to chat?' messages. They are things like 'Those shoes look great with yellow pants and a white blazer.' The screen will then pull up a pic with a model in that outfit with those shoes."

"Wait," said Jane. "That seems like a great idea. But why save this for only new customers? Why not give that prompt for returning customers?"

Jack laughed. "Just you wait," he said with a wink.

"Great question, Jane," Stephen continued. "First, we are trying to get to know the new customer. If she clicks on the pic, we know something more about her. And if she is interested in that outfit, it tells us something about her current and future shoe choices."

Jane was beginning to understand. "Let me guess. You also have pics with other outfits if she doesn't click on that one."

"You got it!" Stephen said beaming. "We have about 50 pics for each pair of shoes we sell. It tells us volumes about the customer. And provides one additional critical opportunity."

Jane sat forward, making a mental guess, and wondering if she was right.

"When the customer goes to make a purchase, she is also able to pick any parts of the wardrobes that she saw and add them to her cart right then. A complete outfit, built around the shoes!" Stephen was proud of himself. Jane was blown away.

"How did you guys do that?"

Jack picked up the dialogue from there. "We work with several clothing partners and hired a talented IT guru to set up the connections. The order is placed with us, each company ships its items, and our system automatically processes payment with each company. In essence, we are buying the items for the customer."

"What about returns?"

"It's effortless," Jack answered. "Because we transferred the purchase through the stores, any returns can be handled directly by that retailer. We've already moved that out of the equation."

"Do you earn a commission?" Jane asked.

"Absolutely," replied Jack. "We earn a small commission. It's pennies, really, in the big picture. But we sell vastly more shoes because of it."

Wow, Jane thought. *This is unique.*

"So, do you offer this for your existing customers?" she asked, assuming they must.

"Yes, we do," Stephen jumped in. "But with even greater clarity. We have a lot of great information about our repeat customers, so we target them a bit differently. We also know what they have purchased before and have a system for continuing to offer them unique selections, overseen by our head stylist. They come to the site, knowing what to expect. They would be disappointed if it was missing."

"This is amazing, gentlemen," Jane said, genuinely impressed.

"There are a few other things we do," Jack said, "including person-alized messages in online sale boxes, and follow-up notes for our in-store customers. There is also always some little surprise, often from one of our vendor partners. A pair of earrings, a pair of men's socks, or a lapel pin. Most of these items we never have to purchase, but they make an incredible impression."

"I bet they do!" Jane said. "Tell me a bit more about this new contract. If a major retailer will now sell your shoes, how will you maintain some of these personal touches?"

"That's our big question, Jane," Stephen said. "We will only have so much control, and many of our personal touches now come because we are the last touch, either in store or from our warehouse. Once we take this contract, many of those things are out of our hands."

"I understand that. It's a challenge for many other retailers who are trying to scale up in a new retail environment. Now let me ask you some more questions to get to the heart of this."

Over the next 30 minutes, Jack and Stephen shared their thoughts and worries, and Jane continued to ask questions, as they seemed appropriate. There were definite challenges, and yet the opportuni-ties were much too great to pass up.

Jack and Stephen answered all her questions readily and began to anticipate some of them as well.

After repeatedly asking them to tell her more and listening to each of their answers, Jane said, "I think we have unpacked all of the vital issues."

Jack and Stephen looked confused.

"That is how I work my strategy. If you noticed, I first asked you to *tell me more*. Then I asked you as many questions as I could think of to see if we have all the pertinent information. I call it *unpacking*, much like a suitcase that is so full that you have to sit on it to zip it up."

They nodded and smiled at the analogy.

"Now that you see all the pieces, what do *you* think are your next steps?"

Jack and Stephen looked a little surprised, not by her question, but because they realized that in the last 30-minutes, they had already come up with many of their solutions. They said as much to Jane, who laughed again.

"You see, that is the beauty of my strategy. Most often, you come up with the answers yourself. I help to facilitate the process. But through my questions, you break down walls, assumptions, and even fears. You begin to look at things through a new lens."

They nodded again, and Jane could see that their brains were on fire. She had felt the same way herself for the past 24 hours. This time with them made her wonder if she should rethink her strategy for her keynote on Friday.

"Jane, we can't thank you enough," Stephen said. "Your dinner is obviously on us," he said, and she nodded acceptance. "But we owe you even more. How long are you in Belfast?"

"I am here until Saturday."

"I promise we'll be in touch before you return to the States."

Business cards exchanged, Jane said her goodbyes and headed back to the hotel. She wasn't sure if it took her three minutes to fall asleep, or two.

Chapter 6

TAXI!

The next morning, Jane woke early again, and couldn't help but wonder how these extra days, meant to be a mini-vacation, were keeping her in a state of creative thought. She had so many thoughts and ideas running through her brain that it was a wonder that she slept at all the night before.

Once she had a cup of coffee in hand, she called her husband, Jeff. He picked up on the first ring, reminding her how much she wished he was with her now.

"Hi, honey!" he said. "How is Northern Ireland?"

"Well, what I've seen of it has been great so far," she said and laughed. "Although it feels like I've barely been out of the hotel."

"It sounds like it from your texts. Tell me about the training yesterday."

"I know it sounds like a crazy thing to do on my day off," she started, laughing again.

"Jane, I know you. You'd give up any vacation day to get a new idea," he said, laughing with her.

"OK, fair enough. But this was something extraordinary. I deal with leadership and sales every day, and although I also talk about customer experiences, I have never had such insight into how to carefully craft a company's mission and vision to achieve it before now. It's clear to me that this hotel has found the perfect intersection of leadership, sales, and customer experience, ensuring that leadership is always focused on building customer experiences that ultimately drive revenue."

"Sounds interesting. I can't wait to hear more about it when you are home."

"Be prepared," Jane said, with mock severity. "You know I will talk nonstop for at least the first hour when I get home."

"Right up until you pass out from exhaustion." He knew her too well.

They visited a few more minutes. Jane was glad she caught her husband in between his meetings and a client dinner. Before they hung up, however, she interjected with one last comment.

"Oh, and honey?" she asked.

"Yes," he replied.

"It's quite likely I'll be bringing home some more shoes."

"Oh, boy. Well, you know the rule." Jane groaned.

"Husband of mine, just because YOU have a rule that one clothing item has to be donated before another comes into the house does not mean that is MY rule," Jane responded, laughing. It was an on-going argument that Jeff was never going to win.

As she hung up, she smiled, ready to face a day as a tourist. All learning would be on hold for a bit.

One of the things Jane was most excited about on this trip was the famous Black Taxi tour. She had heard from many people that it was the only way to truly see Belfast. She hurried down to the lobby to meet Martin, her Black Taxi driver.[12]

Martin had a pleasant smile and warm handshake, and Jane felt immediately comfortable. When he walked her out to the curb and opened the door for her to the rear of the cab, she was surprised that he got in right behind her and took the seat across from her. The taxi had a unique design so that four or maybe six people could ride in the back comfortably, facing each other as if it were booth seating in a restaurant.

"Welcome to Belfast, Ms. Smith," Martin began. "What brings you to our beautiful city?" Jane couldn't help but smile. She loved accents, and Martin's was utterly enchanting.

"I am here to speak at a conference on Friday and wanted to come a few days early to see the city. I am sorry my husband couldn't join me on this trip because he was even more excited than me about taking a Black Taxi tour."

"I am sorry he is not here too, but that just means that you have to return and bring him next time!" Jane smiled, thinking *what a great marketing pitch.*

"You are so right."

"Tell me what you are most interested in seeing today. I want to make sure that we make this experience exactly what you are looking for."

Jane immediately noticed the similarities between the way this experience was beginning and her time at Fred's. What was up with this country?

"Probably, like most people, I am interested in how Belfast has moved beyond the past." Jane began. She wondered if that was the best way to bring up what had to be a touchy subject still, but Martin didn't seem offended and seemed to have expected it.

"Well, I suppose we are moving past by embracing it, to the extent that we can." Martin softly laughed when Jane looked confused.

"Let me explain," he said. "I can go places in my taxi that the tour buses can't go. We don't want the tour buses going through the neighborhoods, though, anyway." Jane nodded.

"If I can show you how personally Belfast was affected, and still is today, you will understand more how sometimes to move forward you have to be willing to look at, and accept the past."

That made sense to Jane. You can't hide problems under the rug, any more than a business could gloss over challenges and threats if they wanted to thrive and grow. There must be moments where you see things you don't want to, to learn how to move forward.

"You'll see that our city and our culture is vibrant. I will take you to places where we are thriving and growing, and show you places where we still have much work to do. In that way, we are not unique."

"I agree," Jane said. "Every country, every place, has some good, some bad, and some in transition. Show me Belfast! I can't wait to experience it."

The day was fun, informative, and harsh at times. Martin took her to a unique spot for lunch: a quiet-looking street with a pub tucked away, that hinted at a lively nightlife. Despite the cold and chill, there were breaks of sun in the sky. She saw people out walking, shopping at corner markets, and a group of men sitting and chatting amicably in a park playing chess.

Martin also took her to the Peace Wall separating the Catholic and Protestant neighborhoods, handed her a marker and told her it was a tradition to write something beautiful on the wall. It seemed both poignant and solemn. She wrote the word LOVE and spent a few moments reading the notes of others.

When they finally pulled back in front of the hotel, Jane thanked Martin.

"Martin, this tour was everything I had hoped to see and learn, and more. Although every experience I've had thus far here in Belfast has been amazing, this gave me a greater appreciation for your country and your people. Thank you."

Martin smiled as he responded. "Jane, it was my pleasure. I love what I do and feel blessed every day to be able to help people understand not only this city, but maybe learn a little bit about themselves as well. We are all human; we are all fallible; we all make mistakes; there are good people and bad. But I like to believe that each one of us can make a positive impact on the world if we choose to."

Jane couldn't agree more and smiled as she walked back into the hotel thinking that, yet again, any customer experience can be significantly impacted by questions that set expectations and don't have the bias of the person transacting the sale.

Once in her room, Jane pulled out her notebook and decided to perform the same exercise on her BLEND strategy on her Black Taxi tour.

B – Be Immediately and Fully Present

Jane had been surprised when Martin climbed in the back of the taxi with her at first, but she wasn't alarmed. He had left the door open, and they were right in front of the hotel. What began as a surprise, however, was proof that the tour was about her, not about him. By not immediately going to the driver seat, his physical presence told her this would be something different. It showed respect for what she wanted in the experience, not just what he, the tour guide, wanted to accomplish.

L – Listen with Your Ears AND Your Eyes

When he moved to the driver seat, Martin kept frequent eye contact with Jane and often pulled to the side of the road to continue with a story or to point out something that he wanted her to be able to take in.

When they got to the Peace Wall, he was quiet. Jane didn't realize it until now, but he must have sensed her awe of the place, and her wish to pay homage to the struggles that had made the wall a necessity.

Even when he handed her the marker and told her to add her message, he left her alone to choose to return to the taxi when she was ready. He waited for it to be her decision. She never felt pressured or pushed to his schedule.

E – Ensure That You Have Asked All the Right Questions

Along the way Martin, asked other questions that, at the time, didn't register as out of the ordinary. But now Jane realized that many of the questions were designed to make sure they didn't miss anything important to her to see. Another example of how, although he likely had a set tour that he could do with his eyes closed, he wanted to ensure that she got what she wanted out of the experience. Even the questions he posed when choosing a place for them to have lunch now took on new meaning, she noted as she reflected.

N – Never Let Your Customer Feel Like a Number

When they returned a few hours later, Jane realized she had never asked how long the tour was supposed to last. Most tours had start and stop time expectations, yet this one flowed with her. Martin gave no impression of needing to rush to the next person. She wondered if Martin would even have another tour that day. But if he did, she never knew it.

D – Deliver an Exceptional Customer Experience (Being Mindful of Financial Return)

There was no doubt Jane had an impactful experience. She tipped Martin well, had bought his lunch, and would recommend the tour, and Martin specifically, to anyone she knew. He had definitely delivered an exceptional experience, at a very reasonable price to her, and she felt confident that she made the day worth his while financially.

After reading her notes, happy with her recap, Jane changed her shoes and decided to walk about the neighborhood. As she strolled the streets with quaint shops and lovely small restaurants, she reflected on her trip thus far. There was something magical here.

On one corner, she found *Don't Burst My Bubble*, a small store with lotions and potions displayed in the windows. She walked in thinking that a bath bomb or some bubble bath would be a great complement to the giant bathtub in her hotel room. A charming tinkling of bells announced her as the door opened.

"Good afternoon!" said a cheery voice from somewhere in the back of the store. "What brings you into my store this glorious afternoon?"

Jane smiled wryly, looking outside at the dripping awnings and a sky that no longer held any hope of sun for the day. A young woman came around a display in a cheery apron carrying a basket.

"Good afternoon," Jane responded. "I was drawn in by your beautiful window display. I am staying at The Prenton and thought I could find something fun to use in the giant tub I have in my hotel room."

As she spoke, the woman returned her smile, nodding as if she fully understood the allure of that clawfoot masterpiece.

"Ah! An American, I presume?" And Jane nodded in response. "I have heard those tubs are gorgeous. I bet we can find just what you need. What do you prefer? Bath bombs? Bath melts? Bubbles?"[13]

"I don't know what a bath melt is. I like bath bombs and bubbles, but I am open."

"Excellent! We need to get you some of each then. My name is Bonnie. What is your name?"

"Jane. Jane Smith," Jane said and shook the hand that Bonnie extended.

"Jane Smith, eh? Is that really your name or are you undercover?" Bonnie asked in an exaggerated whisper and with a conspiratorial wink, making Jane laugh.

"I know. Pretty bland, isn't it? I have my parents to thank for that. I get that question a lot."

"Well, I figured you couldn't be a spy incognito with that fun hair. But you don't hear that name often for a real person. Let's get to the fun part." Bonnie began walking Jane towards the middle of the store.

"First of all, how many days are you here so we can determine how many baths you want to take here and how many wonderful things you want to take home to remember your adventure." Jane loved that approach. What a way to create rapport, learn information and position yourself for an upsell.

"I head back home on Saturday."

"OK. That means four baths here, and enough other goodies to last a week when you return home," Bonnie said, both serious and yet not pushy. She was good. Jane was drawn in further.

Laughing in response, Jane said, "That sounds about right. I always leave room in my suitcase for treasures." Bonnie nodded as if she expected nothing less.

"Tell me, Jane. What kind of scents do you like the most? Herbal? Floral? Spicy? Fruity? Woodsy?" Jane immediately remembered her cocktail adventures with Ken.

"Hm. I would say I am mostly floral and herbal, but fruity sounds fun. What do you have?"

Twenty minutes and a basket of products later, Jane and Bonnie were laughing together, adding a few body lotions to the mix. As they were ringing her up, the tinkling of the doorbell announced another customer. Not breaking stride with Jane, Bonnie made direct eye contact with the new customer. "Good afternoon and welcome!

I'm so glad you stopped in today. Feel free to sniff away. I will be with you in just one moment."

Again, Jane was impressed by the personal attention. Bonnie was able to do two things at once, making both customers feel acknowledged and appreciated. Jane knew she was going to have to write notes about this experience as well.

"Bonnie, thank you for such an amazing experience. I came in for a bath bomb and have left feeling like family. I genuinely appreciate your personal attention."

Bonnie seemed to blush from the compliment. "My pleasure, Jane. I know that people have many choices today on where to shop, and people are making purchases online more than ever. If someone walks in my door, I want to make them feel that there is no place else they could receive such treatment. I want them to embrace the joy of shopping."

"You have done that, and more. I think I'll have to take six baths before I leave to make a dent in all this," Jane said, laughing. "Each time I use one of these products, I will remember you and this store."

The two women shared a hug, and then Jane was out the door, allowing Bonnie to connect with the next customer.

A little further down the road, Jane found a candy store, just as appealing. She stood looking in the window of *Sweet Nothings* trying to fight the urge to give in to her sweet tooth.

Before she could summon her willpower to walk away, however, a man popped his head out the door to smile at her. "Which one is your favorite?" he asked.

Oh boy, thought Jane. *There is no way I can resist that kind of invitation to a candy store.*

"The beautiful chocolates caught my attention. But I see ribbon candy there, and that is one of my weaknesses."

"Then you must come in and taste them!" the man said, holding the door. Jane couldn't help but move towards him.

"We make the ribbon candy in-house, November through January. We have more than 30 flavors and ship all over the world." Jane was in trouble now.

"Thirty flavors? I've only ever had cinnamon and peppermint."

"Then you haven't lived! Please take a seat. Let me show you."

Jane followed the movement of his arm to see that, in the middle of the store, there were five quaint white metal tables and matching chairs with seats covered in red and white striped vinyl. It was reminiscent of an ice-cream parlor from her youth. She found herself sitting down while the man happily chattered and went behind a counter. Within seconds he had candies out on a counter and a plate before him.

"My family has run this store for three generations. My name is Max. What is your name?"

"Hello, Max. My name is Jane."

"Welcome, Jane. Let me give you a candy flight!" He said this with a flourish as he brought her a plate with five single loops of ribbon candy, each on a small doily. This was going to be fun.

"Just as with a wine flight, you want to start with the driest and work your way to sweetest. These are our savory collection. These are candies that are often paired with dishes such as salads or on char-cuterie plates." Jane had never heard of anything like that and was a little hesitant to try.

Max saw her hesitation and jumped in with advice. "Don't feel you need to taste each one. I encourage you to smell them, though. See if any pique your interest. If so, taste it. If not, leave it. You won't hurt my feelings either way."

Jane picked one up and sniffed. It smelled like bacon! The next smelled familiar, but not enough to name it. One smelled distinctly of nuts. Perhaps walnuts. The other two confused her.

She decided to taste the one that smelled like nuts and confirmed that it did, indeed, taste like walnuts. "This is incredible! Walnuts, correct?"

Max nodded, smiling. "Wonderful Jane! Most people have trouble with that one. We have a restaurant in town that requested that flavor. They use it both sprinkled on, and as a garnish, for their wedge salad."

Even though she loved bacon, she wasn't sure she wanted to taste the bacon candy, but she did. Max looked too excited for her to want to disappoint him. She was delighted she did.

"Why bacon flavor, Max? It is delicious, but a little strange," she said, smiling to take away any insult from her words.

"We love strange," said Max. "The more creative, the better. We make another 10 or so flavors for clients that we never sell to anyone else. One restauranteur, in particular, has commissioned us for five exclusive flavors." Jane nodded, seeing how this could be some-thing unique.

"The bacon candy is often served on a charcuterie plate, or as part of the garnish for a Bloody Mary. One restaurant has us create a special form of this to fit on the top of their straws. It is something to behold."

Wow, thought, Jane. *Who knew?*

The flavor she couldn't quite place turned out to be pickle, and the other, two garlic and sweet potato. None were ones that she wanted to take home, but she tasted a bit of each one.

As Max was delivering the next selection, a couple walked in. Not missing a beat, he said, "Enjoy. I will be right back with you."

Jane nodded eagerly and said, "I will be fine, Max. Don't worry about me."

In that short moment, he turned and greeted the couple. "What wonderful confections drove you through the door today?" His smile was infectious, and soon the couple was handed off to someone Jane had not even seen, to sit and sample mints and other goodies for their wedding reception tables. Jane felt, yet again, a sense of being the only customer in the place, and knew the couple felt the same way as well.

Herbal flavors were next and, much like the savory flavors, were used at restaurants and bars throughout the world with specific dishes. They were strange and wonderful, yet not anything Jane would set out at the holidays.

Lightly sweet flavors followed next, more like what she would expect. The quality of the flavors was exquisite, light and airy and simply divine. The final flavors were unique creations, all intense and forward in their scents and flavors. The passion fruit was her favorite, both in taste and color. And of course, Max ended with the traditional fruit, cinnamon, and peppermint.

Jane realized with chagrin that she had tasted every single flavor. And even the tiniest of nibbles added up to a lot. "Max, I have reached my limit for today. Now is the tough part. Deciding what to take with me!"

After boxing up her top favorites, Max handed her another large rectangle box. "What is this?" she asked.

"Jane, you are a very special customer. I want you to remember us here. This box has a piece of every ribbon you tasted today, along with a few new flavors we are trying. Have fun!"

Jane was shocked. "But Max, I only bought a little bit from you. It's too much after all you've given me today." But Max waved off her attempts to hand him back the box.

"I get so much joy sharing my family's legacy. I keep these boxes available for potential large-order customers, and special customers like you." He said, smiling.

"Besides, you allowed me to interrupt your day, forcing you into our store and being gracious enough to try every piece. I want you to have fun sharing this with your husband when you get home."

Jane agreed then. She could see that he meant it. She left, knowing she had to return to the hotel, if for no other reason than to leave her packages there.

When she got back to her room, she couldn't help but examine the box of candy. She opened it up to find a beautiful box with small compartments on each level. Each compartment listed the name of the flavor, and written on the inside of the box was a message:

> *Thank you for spending time with us today. For more than*
> *three generations, our family has created unique and wonderful*

confections here at Sweet Nothings. This sampling of our Ribbon Candy invites you to think beyond your memories and reimagine what candy is. To learn more about each flavor and how they pair with your favorite meals and cocktails, please visit our website.

Just when she thought the experience couldn't be better, she witnessed the marketing value of a simple box of candy. The candy wasn't just to thank her; it was to make her an ambassador.

All because of a simple question: *Which one is your favorite?*

All because of a simple question: *Which one is your favorite?*

An hour later, Jane found herself back at Fred's. It was barely 5:30, and the place was mostly empty, with just a few people at the bar.

Ken smiled as he came her way, and Jane saw Jacqueline wave from across the room while speaking with one of the servers.

"How was your day?" Ken asked as he put a glass in front of her of club soda with lime. It was nice to be a regular. Jacqueline came up before she had a chance to answer.

"It was spectacular!" Jane replied. "Even though I intended to play tourist today, I found myself learning from some other fantastic customer experiences."

When Ken and Jacqueline both said, "Tell me more!" at the same time, they all laughed. Jane had brought a copy of her book for Ken to the training yesterday. She was glad they seemed to be enjoying it.

Jane described a bit of each of her experiences with the Black Taxi tour, and the bath and candy stores. Ken and Jacqueline had been to each, and while they had been talking, Ken began creating a cocktail.

"With everything I have experienced here, I suppose my senses were on high alert for other great experiences," Jane said. "I am excited by the simple ways vastly different businesses can create a memorable customer experience that is also profitable for the business." They both nodded, letting her talk and share her thoughts.

"So often now people are afraid of the death of traditional retail, but I see how any business, service, and product can grow if you are creative, focused and committed to the level of training that will get you there."

At this statement, Ken placed a spectacular cocktail in front of Jane. It was a gorgeous purple that almost matched the color in her hair. On the rim was a butterfly that looked like glass. Upon closer inspection, and after a nod of approval from Ken, she picked it up. It was candy!

"Is this from *Sweet Nothings*?" she asked, excited.

"It is," said Ken. "The moment I heard you went there, I had to make you our signature *Butterfly Pea Tea Martini*."

"Ken, this is stunning! I hope it tastes as good as it looks," she said, laughing. She was not worried about that at all, and her first sip proved it.

Ken smiled at her enjoyment.

"Oh! I forgot to tell you about the shoes!" Jane cried happily, then laughed at the confused faces before her. She told them briefly about meeting Jack and Stephen the night prior.

"You met the owners of *Stepping Out*?" Jacqueline said, shock on her face. Jane nodded in agreement as she sipped her cocktail. She looked at Ken with a glazed over look of satisfaction, only then realizing that both Ken and Jacqueline were looking at her as if she was an alien.

"What's the matter?" she asked. "Why are you both looking at me that way?"

"You had dinner with two of the most famous people in Northern Ireland!" Jacqueline said, dumbfounded while Ken just nodded.

"Oh. Well, we didn't really have dinner. I ate. They had a pint of Beamish and asked for my advice. Are they really that famous?"

"I think you should look them up, Jane." Jacqueline proceeded to start laughing as she pulled out her phone.

It turns out her new buddies were worth quite a lot of money, and made shoes for some very wealthy and famous people. Jane had never been very good at knowing labels.

She said as much, making Ken and Jacqueline laugh even harder.

"But you know what was most impressive about them?" she asked her friends. She continued when they shook their heads no.

"They are more concerned with gaining and keeping regular customers like you and me, than celebrity clients. They have spent a lot of time, money, and energy on ways to ensure that their everyday customer feels a part of something unique. They said they just got a big retail contract. I wonder with who?" Jane asked out loud, making Jacqueline about fall over from laughing.

Jacqueline held up the answer on her phone yet again, and Jane was floored. One of the biggest retailers in the world was about to carry their shoes.

No wonder they are worried about how to scale, Jane thought. *It seems I didn't ask ALL of the right questions.*

Jane ate again at Fred's, this time listening less to the jazz than to the buzzing of her brain. She brought her notebook down from her room, wrote up her notes on *Don't Burst my Bubble* and *Sweet Nothings,* and began to sketch out her next book. Everything she had experienced so far came into play, and she found herself eager to start writing again.

As she said goodnight to Ken and Jacqueline, promising to see Jacqueline again the next afternoon, she decided to change her entire mindset for the trip. She was going to actively seek out great experiences around her, much like the Mystery Shopper that Jack and Stephen described. She thought it might be fun to mix up her presentation on Friday a bit, to incorporate her BLEND concepts.

She even noodled around the idea of sort of persona. Secret Shopper Jane? That sounded fun.[14]

But not as much fun as a giant clawfoot bathtub and a handful of bath melts.

Chapter 7

THE UNSINKABLE MOLTEN CHOCOLATE LAVA CAKE

Early Wednesday morning found Jane at the Titanic Museum, where she spent several hours.[15] She was overwhelmed by the stories told throughout, and by the careful attention to the tiniest details.

She had wondered how she would feel learning so much about such a horrific disaster. The museum made so many things personal that she also felt immediate and direct connection to all who were aboard. Stories were told in letters, pictures, video recreations, and more. She learned about passengers and crew, families and loved ones of those who perished, and the future lives of those that survived. She felt the weight of the tragedy in her body.

Although an emotional and intense morning, Jane was glad that she went. She felt she was honoring the memory of all of the individual lives. Before she went, it was easy to imagine the event in its entirety. The museum broke the story down into millions of pieces:

the people, weather, and building of the ship. Thought had even been given to each chandelier and salt shaker by the creators.

As she walked out, the rain began to fall softly, and she found herself a little melancholy by all she had learned.

Ducking into a small farm-to-table restaurant a few blocks away, she immediately felt centered. A brightly lit fireplace framed the back corner of the open room, and the place was comfortably full with happy, chatting people.

I wonder what Jeff would say if I told him I wanted to remodel our home to include a large hearth, she thought and giggled to herself, imagining the look of horror on his face.

Jane was shown to a small table in the corner, close enough to the fire that she could feel her clothes gently drying, but far enough away not to make her overheat.

Her meal was spectacular in its simplicity: chicken with root vegetables, soda bread, and a bright green salad. She was pleasantly full and felt ready to head back to the hotel to do a little work before meeting up with Jacqueline.

Then it happened.

"I see molten chocolate lava cake in your future."

The voice and the statement shocked Jane from her daydreaming. Her server, Anna, was smiling at her with mischief.

"What?" Jane asked confusion in her voice and likely on her face.

"Imagine a warm dark chocolate cake, filled with a spicy liquid dark chocolate center that spills out as you puncture it with your fork."

Jane was somewhat speechless, and in the gap, Anna continued her torture.

"We dust the cake with powdered sugar, making it look like freshly fallen snow. And we garnish with raspberry puree."

Jane thought she might have begun to drool.

"I would suggest adding a small scoop of our house-made vanilla bean ice cream on the side, as it provides the most wonderful contrast of hot and cold."

This was getting out of hand.

"Our whipped cream, which is to die for, forms a little cloud on the plate, to add as you like."

Jane couldn't even speak.

"Of course, I have many other selections, but based on the dreary day outside, it would be the perfect complement to your meal."

Even dessert followed *BLEND*! You can imagine how it ended. With the added ice cream, of course.

As she returned to the hotel, curious about what she'd learn next, she wondered how Bonnie had become so proficient in sales. Thinking back to her college days waiting tables, Jane knew the value of ensuring your table bought drinks, appetizers and desserts. These high-ticket items were also high profit for the restaurant, and they increased the overall price of the bill, often leading to a larger tip.

But Bonnie took selling dessert to a whole new level. Jane would not have even considered dessert, much less that decadent masterpiece. The description was too much to deny. She had given in, much to the dismay of her comfort.

And yet, it seemed yet one more piece of proof of what she was here to learn.

When Jane found Jacqueline's office precisely at 1:45 p.m., she thought she might need some coffee to keep her from falling asleep. The dessert, while delicious, was probably not the best idea for mental alertness through the rest of the afternoon.

"Hi, Jane!" Jacqueline said, meeting her at the door of her office. "We're going to head right to the conference room. Can I get you anything? Water? Coffee? Tea?

"I would love some coffee. I was just thinking about how wonderful that would be."

"Coming up!" Jacqueline said while she diverted them to a small break room outside the conference room.

Coffee now in hand, they settled in just as Sandra came through the door. "Good afternoon, Jane. I'm glad you could join us again."

"I'm not sure what to expect, but I am ready for anything," Jane responded.

"All set?" Sandra asked Jacqueline.

"Yep. You have your notes, and everyone is ready to go live in three minutes."

Sandra sat down and propped her phone into a tripod.

"Each day at 2:00," Jacqueline began to explain, "an executive team member gives the daily update. Occupancy for the next five days, a reminder of special events, special guests, sales numbers, and something else very special."

Jane nodded. She had introduced many of her clients to this concept. It was called a stand-up meeting, a huddle, a call-to-action, and more. She figured she knew what to expect, but this exact format was new to her.

"What's up with the phone?" Jane assumed it would be a conference call.

"That is how we live stream to all employees. They are all tied-in through another app we use, which they can access on their phones directly. If anyone is with a guest, the event is recorded, and everyone knows they are expected to watch it within 30-minutes of the broadcast."[16]

Interesting, Jane thought. And right then things got started. Jacqueline pulled out her tablet, with the sound off, so Jane could follow along, and opened the app. Jane didn't catch the name of it. It was fun to see Sandra's image on the tablet while sitting close to her as well.

Along the side of the picture of Sandra, Jane could see the names of people checked in and online for the meeting.

"Hello, everyone. Thank you for joining us this afternoon. We are about to begin check-ins for the day. I want to start by congratulating the housekeeping team. I just got word that all of the rooms turning over today were all cleaned and ready for new guests by 1:30 p.m. That is a record!"

Along the comments screen on the side, Jane could see messages of congratulations flying.

"Not only was this done in record time, but we also had a significantly large number of rooms to turn over today. I've asked Norman, the Head of Housekeeping, to tell us how they accomplished this. Norman?"

At that point Sandra clicked a button, allowing Norman to pop on the screen.

"Thank you, Sandra. And thank you, everyone, for your congratulations. As everyone knows, this is something we've been struggling with, especially with some staff turnover we've had recently. I got my team together for a video meeting to brainstorm and included Marsha, the Front Desk Manager, along with a couple of her team members. After all, they are the ones that feel the pain when people are checking in and we don't have rooms available."

"Even though check-in is at 4 o'clock, we know that many guests arrive early. And although we can't guarantee that rooms will be available, we know how much it means to them when one is."

Jane smiled. *Yet another way this hotel was trying to exceed expectations.*

"This was our strategy. We have worked it now for three weeks, trying to perfect it, and today I think we did. A member of the front desk team checks the key drop every 15 minutes, starting at 7:00 a.m. Whenever a guest checks out by key drop, or by the desk, their room number is texted to my manager-on-duty. The manager then works to ensure we are in that room within 15 minutes of notice. It keeps us running, but the heightened sense of urgency has been fun for my team as well."

Wow, Jane thought. It sounded exhausting. She wondered if it was efficient.

"Here's what we have learned: By diving into the history of check-outs, and by watching the up-coming check-ins for people we know are here on business or for conferences, we can adjust our staffing to meet these needs, as well as meet the needs of guests who are not checking out yet. To help that, Marsha came up with another idea that we began implementing a week ago. May I hand it off to her?"

Sandra made a thumbs up comment in the field and switched the presenter to Marsha.

"Thanks, everyone. Working with Norm on this has been fantastic. We knew we had a large group of people here for a conference. When they checked in a few days ago, my team asked each one if they preferred an early or late room cleaning on each day, and if they chose early, we asked them how early they would prefer."

OK, Jane thought. *That is brilliant as long as you can deliver on it.*

"From that list, we knew the exact number that would be out of their rooms by 7:00 a.m., those who preferred no housekeeping, and those who didn't care or wanted later service. We shifted the schedules of the housekeeping staff and turned those rooms over rapidly in between the guests who were checking out."

Sandra took over presenting again. "That is amazing, Norman and Marsha. You both also told me that the housekeeping staff has been enjoying having some choices on flexing their start and end times. I look forward to seeing how these projects progress. And, as always, let us know if any of us can be of help."

Jane figured that entire interchange took less than five minutes. This was exciting. Sandra then went through the numbers.

And less than 10 minutes in, Sandra seemed about to wrap up.

"As always, our last matter of business," Sandra continued, and then picked up a card. "Today we are acknowledging Denny Malton, a new member of the kitchen team. Denny went through training on Monday and yesterday was his first day of work."

Jane looked at Jacqueline, who smiled and nodded yes. We were talking about Denny the dishwasher.

"Denny was recognized by Simon, the Sous Chef for Fred's, who wrote, 'From the moment Denny clocked in, to the moment he clocked out, his positive attitude and work ethic saved us from a stressful evening service. We had a special group of important guests in the private dining room, and everyone in the kitchen was feeling the pressure. Not only did Denny do his job, but he also stepped in to help bus tables when the servers were busy. He didn't ask permission, and he didn't wait to be asked. He saw what was happening and jumped in. He is a great addition to our team.'"

Jane and Jacqueline were smiling with pride, although neither of them was surprised.

"Denny," Sandra continued. "You have demonstrated that you are exactly what we look for in a true team player. Chef Marcos will be presenting you with £50 pounds for your efforts."

Jane was sure Denny was smiling and blushing somewhere.

"And that's it, everyone. Let's continue to make it a great day!"

When Sandra removed her phone from the tripod, and Jane was sure no one was being recorded, she asked, "How many times a month do you do that?"

"Hold the meeting? Every day." Sandra answered.

"No, how many times a month do you highlight an employee and give them cash?"

"Every day," Sandra said with a smile.

"Really? That's quite an investment!"

"Yes, it is. And worth every penny. Sometimes it's a fellow employee who nominates, as in this case. Sometimes it's due to the comments from a guest or vendor. But every single day, 365 days a year, we recognize someone who is fulfilling our mission."

Jane was impressed.

"But there is another devious plan for this as well," Sandra said with a mock evil smile as she leaned in closer. "Even off-duty employees want to know who gets the cash every day. There is a buzz about it the moment the word goes out."

"Are there some people who win a lot? Maybe even too much compared to others?" Jane asked.

"Yes and no. When we see someone who continues to get those kinds of nominations, we believe it is time to do something more than giving them £50 here and there. That is time to consider how to keep them with us over the long term. Perhaps a promotion; perhaps a raise; maybe a special project or assignment. By that time, those people are ready to serve the company at a higher level anyway, so we can offer them another way to be recognized."

"You guys have thought of it all, haven't you?" Jane asked, laughing.

"Never," Sandra answered with a smile in return. "If we think that, then we will start to go backward. We want to constantly be looking for new and better ways, never getting complacent. But I know Jacqueline is going to share our most powerful tool in just a moment.

That, I believe, is the game-changer for us and for any other company that chooses to employ it. On-going training is never static." And with that, Sandra excused herself to head to a meeting.

"Are you ready?" Jacqueline asked, smiling.

"Ready as I can be," responded Jane.

Chapter 8

READING, WRITING, AND ARITHMETIC

Jane didn't know what to expect as Jacqueline moved to the seat Sandra had just vacated and connected her tablet to the massive wall monitor.

The screen showed Jacqueline's desktop as she opened the app they had used for Sandra's broadcast. It was called TrainRS.

"Jane, so far you have been privy to two of our training tools. All new hires go through the same orientation you attended on Monday. All on-duty staff are expected to view the daily management broadcast live, within 60 minutes of the live broadcast, or before beginning their shift," Jacqueline began. "As we told you, nearly all of the staff views the daily broadcast, even if they are off duty, although we do not require that. We know that many of them do, however, due to the admin tracking functions in the app."

Jane nodded, and Jacqueline continued.

"We take care to ensure that the management broadcast never exceeds 10 minutes. The timing is critical for attention, as well as planning."

Jane appreciated that. Time was money, but keeping people's attention was even more critical. Short, sweet, and to the point.

"Mostly," Jacqueline continued, "the daily update is just a refresher. Each staff member has also already received the sales and occupancy data on their phones before the broadcast."

That surprised Jane, and prompted her to ask, "Isn't that redundant?"

"Great question. We know that people learn and absorb information in a variety of ways. We want every team member to know the vital financial and occupancy data daily, so we use several methods for ensuring that."

Jane was impressed and excited to see what else was to come. She nodded to Jacqueline to indicate that she was following.

"The initial live training is a vital tool, but the heart of our ongoing training happens through the TrainRS app," Jacqueline said, clicking on the app. The screen popped up with a course called *Greeting New Guests*.[17]

"In addition to the day-long live training, every new employee also goes through a 12-week app-based training program, receiving course instruction and evaluation every day. The courses build on the core competencies for their position, provide opportunities for them to proactively receive additional training and coaching, introduces them to our benefits programs, and more."

Wow! Jane thought. She had created something similar for a client several years ago, and it had been a big hit. But it had only been for one position in their company. Jacqueline was telling her they had created these programs for every single job!

While she was talking, Jacqueline scrolled through the course, which didn't seem overly burdensome. It seemed to be rather short, and she said as much to Jacqueline.

"Yes, it is short," Jacqueline agreed. "The first three weeks of any position are very stressful for a new employee. We are throwing a lot of information at them, with a lot of on-the-job training. No course in the first three weeks is longer than 10 minutes."

That made sense to Jane. Why add more stress than you had to? Get them comfortable with the process of daily lessons by building up in length.

"You want to give them enough training, but not so much they can't handle it," Jane said.

"Exactly," Jacqueline responded. "These first courses are simple, and many are common sense, but we want to prepare them for what is to come."

Jane nodded for Jacqueline to continue.

Meanwhile, Jacqueline pulled up another course called *Weekly Recap.*

"Each Friday," Jacqueline continued, "every department manager completes an evaluation of each of their team members who are in their initial 12 weeks. Managers evaluate them on the core lessons they completed, timeliness, professionalism, attire, and more. New employees also recap the week's courses, evaluate themselves on the core issues their managers rate them on, and provide feedback on their training for the week. It takes about 15 minutes to complete, again trying to maximize and conserve time. Once both parties have completed this step, they are each given access to data from the other. It is a blind process until both are done."[18]

"Jacqueline, this is incredible. This allows you to adapt training along the way during the critical probation period of a new employee."

"Absolutely," Jacqueline agreed, nodding. "It also allows us to see if we have missed any steps in the training process. It isn't fair to get a new hire to the end of probation only to find out we missed critical elements along the way. That ultimately harms the employee and the company."

"You know," Jane said, "training was the biggest challenge in my last position as a vice president of sales. With hundreds of people and hundreds of stores across the country, we relied a lot on on-the-job training and hoped the manager was hitting all the important elements. But we never knew for sure how good our training was unless we saw great successes or great failures. This sounds like you can track it even better."

"We not only track it, Jane, we know where the employees stand with every course, in every day and every week of their employment."

At Jane's perplexed look, Jacqueline went to the admin function of the app and pulled up the course they had just reviewed. But instead of course materials, she saw raw data.

"We implemented this course about a year ago. All staff, new and current, were required to take it. By the way, I don't think I mentioned that tenured employees take one or two courses per week. Continual learning and development is part of our culture."

Jane thought that might be an understatement as Jacqueline looked back again to the monitor.

"What you see here," she said, illustrating with a laser pointer, "is the average time to complete the course, the time spent on each question, and the number of right and wrong answers. If you look at it closely, you can see those who cheated."

Jane could see that it took people, on average, seven minutes to complete the course. None took longer than 12, and many went as quickly as five. But one person completed the course in two minutes.

"Interestingly," Jacqueline said, "when the course came out, this employee was in review for underperformance. There were several warning signs that she was not the right match for the company, and this proved it. She was four weeks into the position, was not responding well to coaching on the areas that needed improvement, and was exhibiting attitude problems. With this last data point, we found the confidence to make a change."

Now that impressed Jane. Many of her clients struggled with what to do with an underperforming new hire. In many cases, they had not trained the employee well enough, but in just as many cases, the employee was the problem. More often than not, the company, uncomfortable with cutting a loss early, would move the person on after probation only to have to terminate them later.

"Our training programs have data behind them for department managers, and they are required to act on it. Sandra and I review their training programs weekly and adapt the managers' training as well, as needed. Some of them need help learning to coach underperforming employees; some need support finding balance and delegation; others need to work on their communication skills. Every employee here, including Sandra and myself, have a dedicated training program designed for our positions."

"Who creates the plans for you and Sandra?" Jane asked, surprised.

"Great question. First, Sandra and I meet with the CEO of the hotel quarterly, and she, along with the Board Chair, review and recommend training and development for Sandra and me. Most of what we do comes from external trainings, conferences, and associations, but we still put the training into coursework in case either of us isn't here tomorrow."

"Now that," Jane said, "is something I have never heard of, and yet is such a stunning idea. That is true succession planning, isn't it?" Jacqueline nodded.

"Second, Sandra and I complete a monthly evaluation on each other via the app, just as department managers do with their tenured employees and that Sandra and I do with them. No one escapes the opportunity for review."

"Isn't that a lot of work? I have trouble getting my clients to do performance reviews annually for their employees. You are conducting 360 reviews every month?" Jane couldn't imagine any of her clients considering that.

"Yes, we really do it once a month. It isn't a lot of work when you are doing it continually. Each month we include questions similar to those we talked about with the new hires — professionalism, timeliness, etc. Every month also has a theme. November's theme is on mutual respect, and December's is on cultural sensitivity. Each August we focus on professional development so we can identify additional training resources we may want to include in the next year's budget."

"One more thing," Jacqueline added, making Jane laugh, and Jacqueline smile.

There must be more than one thing given Jacqueline's enthusiasm, Jane thought.

"Any employee who must attain or maintain a certification, like our kitchen staff and bartenders, can complete any required coursework through the app."

That brought Jane's attention back again. "Really? Aren't those state-regulated?"

"Yes, most of them are. We showed the accrediting agencies our training program, used their materials, paid the required fees, and proved that employees completed them during their work time. That was a big plus."

It certainly is, thought Jane. The agencies still got their money but could be even more confident that coursework is being completed thoughtfully and with full employer support.

"In fact," Jacqueline continued, "two of them have been working with us to see how to adapt this app to their systems. We input an incoming employees' certification data and, before they expire, the app sends a push notification to the employee, their manager, and me. All three of us work in tandem to make sure recertification happens with no gaps."

With this, Jacqueline pushed back a bit from the table as if to say, *what do you think?*

"Jacqueline, I thought I was impressed on Monday. This is something else altogether. I have seen companies with impressive new hire training programs. I have seen companies who diligently test and train on new products and services. But I have never seen a training program like this, especially in the hospitality industry."

"Thank you. We work very hard to create and maintain a level of excellence, not only for our guests but for our employees. People who feel they have been trained well feel more confident in their positions and their employer. We not only expect great things in terms of our mission; we are also creating a culture that values education, training, development, and continual improvement. As Sandra told you on Monday, our efforts are resulting in substantially lower turnover rates and significantly higher rates of internal promotions. All these things together create stability."

 People who feel they have been trained well feel more confident in their positions and their employer.

"I have no doubts," replied Jane.

Jacqueline began to disconnect her phone, and Jane made a request. "Jacqueline, I have a huge favor to ask of you. Would you and Sandra be willing to come to my presentation on Friday at the spa conference, along with Ken? I know I'm asking a lot, and I am happy to pay for your time. I want to get your feedback on my presentation as well as highlight The Prenton. I'll be at the convention center, speaking from 3:00 to 4:30 p.m."

Jacqueline went right to her phone, typed something in, and turned back to Jane. "Sandra's schedule was clear, and I just adjusted all of our calendars so that we can come. I'll let Sandra know when she is out of her next meeting. I'm sure both she and Ken will be as excited as I am to see you in action. And there is no need to cover any of our time. This sounds like a public relations event!"

Back in her room, Jane called her contact for the presentation Friday, to confirm last-minute details as well as make a request. Johanna picked up the phone on the first ring.

"Hello, Jane!" she said. "I was just about to call you. Everything is set on our end for you on Friday. The conference has been going great so far. We have our biggest turnout ever, and everyone is excited to hear from you."

"Wonderful! I am just as excited, and I have a question for you, Johanna."

With Johanna's clearance to ask away, Jane continued.

"The past few days have been very enlightening here in Belfast. Would it be all right if I changed my presentation to reflect some ideas that will be even more beneficial to your group?"

"Jane, you know I am a big fan of yours. I would listen to anything and everything you have to say, and I know the group will as well. Please feel free to make any changes. You can email me new slides up to an hour before you are onstage Friday or bring new slides on a thumb drive and we can upload them right before you speak."

"Thank you, Johanna! I appreciate the trust and flexibility. I'll have updated slides to you tomorrow evening so that you will have plenty of time to get them to the AV team."

With that, Jane settled in for an evening of work, room service, and an early night. But first, she went down to Fred's for a few moments to ask for some props and some help from her buddy Ken.

Chapter 9

ENYA AND CHANTING

Weeks before leaving for Europe, Jane figured that she needed to do some rigorous research in the spa industry. She pre-booked an appointment for a facial at one of the Belfast's top spas, and as she walked up to the door Thursday morning, she wondered briefly if this could be considered a business expense. She doubted her accountant would agree.

Jane's definition of a great facial was one where she fell asleep. Once she made it past the torture of the extractions, she usually settled into a peaceful and meditative state. If she had to ask the esthetician later if she had been purring (she would never call it snoring), it was an exceptional experience.

As she walked in the front door, Jane noticed a large, cheerful, and plentiful gift shop. Lotions, potions, candles and clothes were artfully arranged. She was momentarily confused by two desks on either side of the room but quickly decided check-in must be with the ladies in spa attire. The other desk was staffed with people in business attire.[19]

Bright smiles from three women greeted her as she stepped to the desk, and one of them spoke out.

"Hello! My name is Bethany. Are you checking in for an appointment this morning?"

What a great question, thought Jane. *It makes me feel welcome.*

Whenever Jane went somewhere for an appointment of any kind, she always felt like the question, "How can I help you?" made her feel the need to justify her presence. It was uncomfortable and awkward. But this direct question was inviting and welcoming.

It was also endearing to have Bethany share her own name first. That made it even more personal.

"Yes, I am. My name is Jane Smith, and I have an appointment at 10 o'clock for a facial."

Bethany smiled, looked at her computer without losing more than a few seconds of eye contact, and said, "Wonderful! We were expecting you, Jane. We have you scheduled for our Adaptive Facial. Is that correct?"

Jane nodded, agreeing.

"Jane, you are going to love this facial. The esthetician can adjust it to your specific needs and goals as she goes along. We have you with Mary-Kate. She is fabulous!"

Jane thought about how well Bethany had just framed her upcoming experience. She validated Jane's choice in the service, gave a glowing review of Mary-Kate, and let her know a little about what to expect. She couldn't help but smile at the little ways the spa and its team were already giving her a great customer experience, and more material proving her BLEND strategy.

Jane was shown to the women's locker room, given a tour, a locker and a robe, and then left to her own devices. She had about 20 minutes before her appointment to enjoy the steam room.

Sitting in the spa waiting room, waiting for your provider, is an uncomfortable experience. There are usually several people waiting for their treatment provider to come in, announce their name, and take them off to receive pampering.

It always reminded Jane of being young, waiting to be picked for a dodgeball team, or other school P.E. activity. Jane was never picked first, always afraid she would be picked last, and often ended up somewhere in the middle. Sports weren't her forte.

As each treatment provider came in, everyone seemed to feel the heightened anticipation of being "next." Soon all the women were taken, and Jane was wondering if she had been forgotten. That happened to her once. And then, Mary-Kate walked in.

Mary-Kate walked over with her hand out and said, "You must be Jane." She had a great smile, and Jane rose to shake her hand and assure her that she was, indeed, Jane.

To Jane's surprise, Mary-Kate motioned for her to sit again for a moment. *This is unusual*, thought Jane. *I hope this doesn't run into my facial time.*[20]

As if reading her thoughts, Mary-Kate said, "Jane, you have only the one treatment today, correct?" Jane nodded, yes.

"Wonderful. Your appointment is for 65 minutes. I schedule them for that amount of time so that we have a few extra minutes to prepare for your facial. Is that all right?"

Hm, Jane thought. *I have a feeling this experience might not be what I expected. I wonder what more I will learn today.*

After Jane assured her that the plan was fine with her, Mary-Kate continued.

"Jane, what made you decide on a facial today?"

"Great question, Mary-Kate," Jane responded. "I try to get facials a couple of times a year. It's been a while, and it seemed like a good gift for myself as we head into the heart of winter."

"Very smart. Most people don't think about how the changes in weather affect their skin. Do you have any particular challenges with your skin that I should know about?"

"Well, one main thing, I suppose. I am a speaker, and I travel constantly. Between airplanes and stage lights, my face can look a little ruddy. I also tend to have oily skin in spots, but I try to take excellent care of my face. I'm curious what you have to say after you've seen it up close and personal, however, only you will know whether I am successful." Jane and Mary-Kate laughed at this together, and Jane felt even more at ease.

"Wonderful. My last question is this: What kind of experience do you enjoy most during your facial? Do you appreciate complete peace and quiet, or would you like to know a bit about what I am doing through the process?"

This is even more adaptive than I thought, mused Jane.

Floored by the question, Jane immediately thought of how shrewd this was. Mary-Kate was going to literally cater her service to Jane's wishes.

"Wow! What an interesting question. No one has ever asked me that before."

"I think it's important not to assume," said Mary-Kate. "Just because someone comes to the spa doesn't mean that everyone wants Enya and chanting."

This made Jane laugh out loud. "You're right. And usually, I do enjoy that. It is such a contrast to my daily life. But I think today I'd like to know about what you are doing along the way. I am excited to be an active participant."

"In that case," said Mary-Kate, rising from the couch, "Let's get started. I am confident that you will enjoy this."

Once settled under the covers, enjoying the warmth of the heated facial chair, Jane was ready. Still lulled by the gentle spa music in the background and the scent of lavender and lemon in the air, Mary-Kate began softly describing everything that she did.

"Jane, I am going to begin by cleansing your face. I am using a gel cleanser. I chose this product because although you told me your skin tends to be oily, I can also see that your skin is a bit dehydrated, probably from your recent flight. How often do you fly?"

"Almost every week," Jane replied.

"I thought as much. When we finish today, I am confident that you will see the benefit of additional moisture from non-oil-based products."

A few minutes later, Jane was preparing against the barrage that comes along with extractions. But to her surprise, Mary-Kate had a few tricks up her sleeve.

"Jane, in a minute I am going to put steam near your face to open your pores for the extractions. Before that, however, I am going to apply lip balm to your lips." Jane was glad she had advanced warning of this because it could have shocked her. No one had ever applied lip balm to her lips before in a facial, and she often felt them dry out through the process.

"Given the fact that your skin is already a little dehydrated from your flight, your lips are as well, and they are a lot more sensitive to the steam." Jane mumbled something that sounded like understanding.

"And to prepare and protect your eyes, I am going to do two things. First, am applying cotton pads with a lemongrass and rosewater solution that will soothe this tender skin and brighten the bit of darkness there from your jetlag."

Man, Jane thought. *I can't hide anything from her.* But she knew it was true and didn't feel the least bit insulted.

"Then, I am going to put a pair of those glasses that people wear in tanning booths. I know the light can be bright and very uncomfortable. More importantly, I want to ensure that we are protecting your eyes."

Jane was thrilled about this addition. The brightness of the light was very uncomfortable.

The rest of the treatment was blissful, and Jane smiled as she heard things she wanted to commit to memory for use in her presentation the next day.

"Jane, you have lovely skin. I suspect, however, that you have to manage your pores very carefully. I am going to use a toner that will both calm and tighten them. Let me know what you think as I apply it."

Jane couldn't deny the comment about her pores. She had always struggled with them, but never really knew what to do about them. By Mary-Kate recognizing it, as well as providing a solution, Jane was already more eager to try, and likely buy, the product if it did what Mary-Kate promised. It was a slam-dunk sales technique.

"I'm going to end today with a weightless UV defense sunscreen. It won't feel heavy on your skin, and it will give you great coverage."

Again, Jane was impressed by Mary-Kate's ability to identify one of Jane's challenges and present a solution in a manner that could easily lead to a sale. Jane spent much of her youth not wearing sunscreen on her face because the lotions were too heavy for her skin.

When the facial was over, and Jane joined Mary-Kate in the hall, she was in for one last surprise.

The moments after a facial are somewhat surreal. You have to make the disappointing transition from the warm chair and relaxed state back to the real world. When you open the door, your esthetician greets you, standing there like an honor guard, glass of water in hand, ready to escort you back to the locker room.

Sometimes the esthetician will hand you a card listing all of the products used on you that you can purchase in the spa shop. Sometimes you are just quietly walked back, and bid farewell, while the treatment provider hurries off to prepare for the next guest.

Both scenarios always seemed like a letdown to Jane. The salesperson in her was always looking for an attempt to secure ancillary sales. And because this hardly ever happened, Jane very rarely bought any products after a facial.

Jane knew that there was a fine line between sales and a spa experience and that not everyone possessed a sales mindset as she did.

She was continuously dissecting sales opportunities to see business potential. But when people shy away from asking someone to make a purchase, the answer will always be no.

 When people shy away from asking someone to make a purchase, the answer will always be no.

This time, however, she was in for a treat. Before being led away from the room Mary-Kate started to hand Jane the product card, but instead of letting go, held on to it gently and said: "Jane, I used several products on your skin today, and I want to make sure you have a complete list to refer to."

Jane nodded, enjoying this moment. She was confident that Mary-Kate would not disappoint her as others had before her.

"Your eyes drank up this eye cream," she said first, pointing to the product. "They looked brighter, almost immediately."

That caught Jane's attention. She never really thought about how the esthetician could *see* the effects of the facial. She had only ever thought before about how the facial had *felt* to her.

"Also, I know you said your skin was looking a little ruddy before we started." Jane nodded, impressed by how Mary-Kate was pulling this all together. "When you look in the mirror, you will see the immediate effect of the Vitamin C serum that I used on your skin. You have a healthy glow now."

Jane was impressed. But she was even more impressed when Mary-Kate said, "You can buy all of these products in the spa shop," as she pointed to the entire list with her finger, "but I know you will benefit from these two products in particular." She said while pointing out the Vitamin C serum and the eye cream.

"Mary-Kate," Jane began, "may I ask how you got so good at sales?"

Mary-Kate looked at her quizzically. "Sales? I'm not a salesperson. I just know that you will like those products."

With good wishes on both parts, Jane returned to the dressing area and went straight for the mirror. There was no doubt about it. Her skin and eyes looked brighter and healthier.

I wonder if I would have even noticed if Mary-Kate hadn't pointed it out.

Twenty minutes and £100 in products later, Jane headed happily back to the hotel with even more material for her presentation the next day. It looked like she was going to have to make even more last-minute adjustments to her slides.

Chapter 10

SHAKEN OR STIRRED?

The moments before Jane went onstage were always fun. There were feelings of butterflies, nervousness, and eagerness to get started all mixed happily together. She remembered her first time speaking in front of a large crowd. She was in the sixth grade and had been one of two students chosen to receive the key to their brand-new school building.

To this day, Jane didn't know why she was chosen, and she couldn't remember what she said, but she knew that after commanding an audience of 600 or so people, she was hooked on public speaking. She liked to entertain and educate in equal portions.

And now it was showtime. Johanna began to introduce her from the stage.

"Ladies and gentlemen, I know you are all as excited as I am to hear our keynote speaker. You have all read Jane Smith's book, *Tell Me More: How to Ask the Right Questions and Get the Most Out of Your Employees*. And any that didn't do their homework will see me after school." Johanna paused for dramatic effect and the expected laughter. "Although she is going to reinforce those messages, she also has something new to share with us. So, without further ado, please welcome Jane Smith!"

Jane walked out under the bright lights to applause and smiles and was ready to get to work.

"Thank you, everyone! It is such a pleasure to be here with you all today. I know you've had a few power-packed days and are ready to head home tomorrow to implement all you have learned."

Heads nodded in agreement as Jane continued.

"We are here to talk about leadership today. But I want you all to reflect on the fact that you all run sales companies. In each of your spas around the world, you are responsible for sales. Sales of your services; sales of your products; and sales of your reputations. Would you agree?"

More heads nodded and agreement was verbalized throughout the auditorium.

"Today, we are going to talk about the symbiosis between leadership and sales to create an exceptional customer experience."

Although it is difficult to see people from the stage in a room with 4,000 people, Jane felt their anticipation of her message.

"How many of you are absolutely certain that while you are here this week for this conference, your team is back at home delivering exceptional customer experiences while also increasing your top-line sales?"

The sounds in the audience were not as overwhelmingly positive as they had sounded just moments before.

She let the question hang there, discomfort beginning to grow, when she hit them again with the next question.

"How many of you are certain that every member of your team is as committed to the financial success of your business as you are?"

The furtive sounds of people shifting uncomfortably in their seats was deafening against the silence. And silence was never the norm in a room with 4,000 people.

"And how many of you can raise your hands right now and say that the exceptional customer experiences that they deliver are quantifiably related to product sales, repeat business, and direct referrals?"

The mumbling became nervous again, and Jane couldn't see any raised hands.

"I know many of you. I have worked with some of your spas and know that you hire quality professionals. You are diligent about making sure your teams are current with all certifications and trained on new treatments. You train your teams well."

Heads nodded all around.

"So don't be dismayed by your reactions to my questions," Jane said with a smile, and her arms spreading wide as if to prepare to embrace them all. "I have the answer for you. And I promise you that you will leave here today with the strategy to make this a reality in your spa. Are you interested in learning more?"

Now everyone was fully engaged.

"We often look at our critical business elements in silos." As she spoke, a slide began to build on itself, beginning with one circle with the words Therapists & Treatments in the middle.

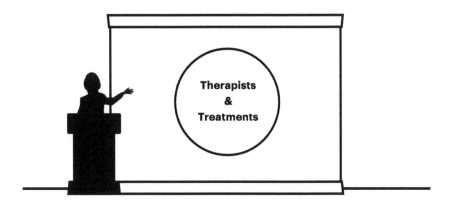

"We need quality and certified therapists who are also up on current treatments, so we spend a lot of focus on this area of education. After all, this is our bread and butter, right?"

Murmurs of agreement filled the room.

Now another circle with the words Receptionists & Products in it.

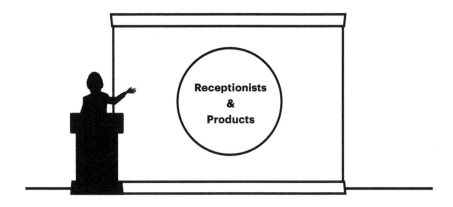

"We hire these people to provide the services, and we teach the desk staff to sell products, correct?"

More agreement.

"We train our desk staff to answer the phone and book appointments. We train them to mail out cards to customers we haven't seen in a while. We train them to ask for referrals. We spend a lot of money on advertising to bring in new customers."

As she spoke, more circles appeared with the following words: Appointments, Phones, Customer Retention, Referrals and Advertising.

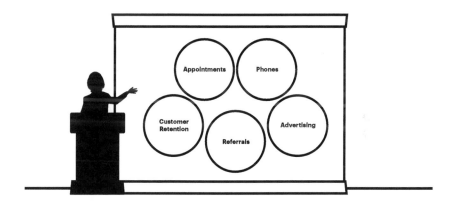

Jane leaned out on the stage as if to whisper a secret.

"So why don't we sell more product? Why don't we see more, and frequent, repeat business? Why don't we see more direct referrals? Why do we constantly spend money on advertising to bring in new customers?"

Jane could feel the tension building, and smiled inside. She did that on purpose.

One of the strategies Jane liked to employ when she spoke was to ask enough questions that people had to think. And often that made them a little uncomfortable. That was alright with her. She knew that growth came from discomfort. It very rarely came from a place of ease.

So she hit them again, just when they thought they knew where she might be going next.

"How many people on your teams consider themselves 'salespeople?'"

More nervous noises filled the room. Jane was quiet for a few seconds as she let the question hang in people's minds.

"I have a little secret to share with you," Jane said, leaning out towards the audience, speaking in an animated whisper.

"With the right BLEND between leadership, sales and the customer experience, you can infuse new life and company commitment into your team. Would you like me to *tell you more*?"

As Jane emphasized those three words, she got the laughs and nods of agreement she was expecting. It was time to let them off the hot seat for a bit.

Jane put up a picture with a dog relaxing at the spa, generating laughs through the room.

"This is your ideal customer," Jane said over the laughter. "Happy, relaxed, and about to take home a lovely assortment of products while planning a return trip with 10 of her best friends."

The next two slides followed her points perfectly.

Jane was enjoying the moment, knowing that she had her audience fully engaged.

"But there is only one way to ensure that this ideal customer moves from a happy client to client who purchases product, becomes a repeat customer, *and* makes referrals," Jane continued.

"Your leadership must include both constant training and an unwavering commitment to getting your team on board for success. You must infuse the right *BLEND* in your business."

"In the beauty industry, blending is usually about beauty products. Lotions, potions, and bath salts, right?" People nodded throughout the room.

"Our goal at this conference is to create exceptional experiences while also increasing sales of our beauty products, correct?"

Heads nodded again as people were anxious to see where this was heading.

"But we seem to be missing the perfect recipe for both, wouldn't you say?" Even despite the stage lights, she could tell the group was enthusiastically involved.

"I am here to tell you, however, that the most potent sales and customer experiences do indeed follow a recipe for success. And I've found it."

"This week, I have been staying at The Prenton Hotel, and have been fortunate enough to be privy to the inner workings of their mission and training strategy. This is a business that is dedicated absolutely to the symbiotic purpose of creating exceptional experiences while delivering financial success. I have invited the director of training and the general manager to join us today in the audience. Jacqueline and Sandra, will you please stand up?"

It took the room a moment to pinpoint the two women in the crowd, but as they stood and gave a quick wave, the audience gave them welcoming applause.

"I developed my BLEND recipe as a direct result of watching these women and their company in action. They've also allowed me to share their core mission with you and, as you will see in a few moments, it is the foundation for BLEND."

At this statement, Jane put up a slide that read *The Prenton's Core Principles*:

- The customer, and their experience, *always* comes first.

- No one person or one position is more important than creating and maintaining an excellent customer experience.

- Each day you will be expected to find ways to deliver on our first promise, while also building the financial success of the company.

"I was the fortunate recipient of these principles from the moment I walked into the hotel, and into Fred's Cocktail and Jazz Club. I know for a fact that The Prenton team delivers on these promises every day. I was fortunate enough to participate in a number of their training programs. And I can tell you this for certain. The difference between their success and yours has to do with the intersection of vision, leadership, training and development. It has to do with how they blend these important areas together.

Another graphic came up with each of those words in circles, with the word BLEND at the intersection. — vision, leadership, training, development

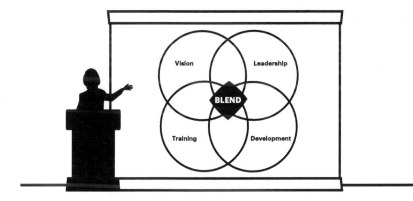

"The Prenton takes training and professional development very seriously, from the interview and hiring process, to the initial in-person new hire training, to ongoing, daily methods for training and nurturing the skill-set of their employees," Jane said, making sure she was keeping everyone's attention. "They do not leave things up to chance, and they do not follow the 'train-the-trainer' methodology. They believe in going directly to the front-line employees, daily, to ensure that everyone operates at their highest potential."

"To that end, and with their permission, I have taken their concepts and created a recipe just for you. This recipe must be rooted in training. This is not a PowerPoint that you can share with your team when you return home and hope that it will magically impact your bottom line."

"This recipe, this blend for success, requires vision on your part to see how it can and should impact your company. It requires leadership that doesn't waver, and that doesn't treat it like a fad that could be replaced tomorrow. It requires training, initially and on-going, allowing your team to embrace it throughout many aspects of the company and their career. And this recipe requires you to invest in the professional development of your team."

With that, she put up a Slide that listed the BLEND strategy:

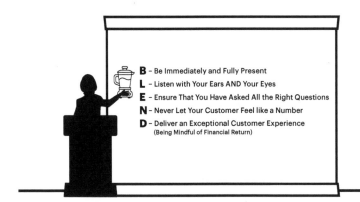

While people lifted their phones to take pics of the slides, Jane continued. "Both the guiding principles from The Prenton, and my BLEND recipe require an intersection of leadership, training, and professional development that takes us from silos to collaboration."

Jane could see that people were intrigued and wished she had enough time to share all the training tools used at The Prenton, but she also thought she should let Jacqueline and Sandra share that if they wanted to. She still had some points to drive home. Plus, there were likely some residual training opportunities for her in this.

"Now, don't fret about the slides. Johanna will make sure you have them after the event, and I will shamelessly plug myself after the presentation as well." Chuckles from around the room created the perfect opportunity for one last surprise of the program.

"So let's see how tasty this recipe is. May I have my assistant on stage please?" As Jane motioned to the side of the stage, Johanna pushed out a rolling cart covered with a cloth and several mysterious items underneath. People were giggling softly, wondering what was to come.

"May I have a hand for my lovely assistant Johanna?" Jane said, smiling while Johanna made a Vanna-like arm sweep of the cart and walked off stage in beauty-pageant form.

Sweeping off the cloth, Jane revealed martini glasses, a cocktail shaker, and bottles and jars in various sizes, displayed clearly on the large monitors to each side of the stage.

"You may be wondering what this is all about," Jane said while the audience laughed. "It is 5 o'clock somewhere," she drawled, gaining even more laughter.

"I need a volunteer from the audience, please. Someone who enjoys a good martini." Hands shot up from around the room while she pretended to survey the group with a critical eye. She loved building tension.

Finally, she gave in. "You there in the front row with the green jacket." Jane indicated, and the man shot up quickly to come on stage.

"What is your name?" Jane asked.

"Bob Sheppard," Bob replied.

"Nice to meet you, Bob. Where are you from?"

"I am from Nashville, Tennessee," Bob replied, followed by catcalls and cheers from the audience. Clearly, there were others from Nashville in the room.

"I love Nashville!" said Jane. "Bob, thank you so much for not only volunteering but for sitting in the front row. You have no idea how sad it makes me when people are afraid to be too close to me," she said with a laugh.

"I am assuming you like cocktails, Bob?" Bob nodded enthusiastically.

"Excellent. What is your favorite type of martini, Bob?"

"I'm a simple man," Bob said while holding out the lapels on his bright green jacket. The group knew him well given the number of chuckles that followed his statement.

"So, I am a classic dirty martini kind of guy."

"Perfect. I am a fan myself. I am not a good bartender, however," Jane said, making Bob appear confused. "And I want to make sure I can focus on you and not attempt a job I am not trained for."

With this statement, a slide went up saying:

"Thankfully, I know someone who is a great bartender. I'd like you to all meet Ken, lead bartender and another member of The Prenton team. Ken, would you mind coming to join us please?"

Ken walked out, pristine in his leather apron and trademark white shirt and purple tie, waving at the crowd that was coming alive now. Jane introduced Ken and Bob, who shook hands before Ken went behind the traveling bar to get to work.

"Tell me, Bob," Jane asked. "Do you prefer your martini shaken or stirred?" Her attempt at a 007 accent made people groan.

"I have no idea. I just order them, and they come," Bob said, looking a bit uncertain

Jane put up another slide then, stating:

"Bob," Jane said, "That is no problem. I bet Ken can help us with a solution.

Ken nodded and chimed in. "Bob, do you like it when your martini has little chips of ice in it?"

"Yes."

"Then you prefer them shaken," Ken responded while adding ice cubes to the shaker.

Bob looked pleased that he had learned something new.

"Do you prefer gin or vodka?" Jane asked.

"That is easy. I prefer vodka."

"Excellent," Jane said. "Do you have a brand you prefer?"

"I prefer Stoli, but anything will do if you don't have that."

The room "ooh'd" though when Ken pulled a bottle of Stoli from under the cart and poured some into the shaker. Bob smiled.

"Bob, how do you feel about vermouth? Do you like a very dry martini?" Jane continued. She had to admit to herself that it was lucky that Bob liked a martini she actually could make.

"Hm. I don't know. No one has ever asked that of me. I suppose I do like it dry, but not so dry it makes me pucker." Bob made a funny slapping sound and motion with his tongue. The audience was eating this up.

"Bob, I will use a brief spray of dry vermouth then, to wash the glass," said Ken. "That should be perfect for what you are looking for." Bob nodded his assent.

"Finally," Jane continued, "How dirty do you like your dirty martini Bob?" Everyone in the room laughed at this, and Jane realized she might have gotten a little red in the face. It was too good of a joke opportunity not to take, however.

"Great question," Bob said, laughing along with Jane and the room. "I just like a hint of the olive juice. Too much is overwhelming, especially if I have it with dinner."

With this, Ken nodded and added a couple of dashes of brine to the shaker. In seconds the shaker was being used for just that. Ken poured the concoction into a glass and garnished with a skewer with olives and handed the glass to Jane while Bob looked on, eagerly awaiting his prize.

But Jane had something else in mind.

"A perfectly created and customized martini," Jane said, holding the glass so it could be displayed on all the monitors. "Does it look delicious Bob?" she asked.

"It looks perfect!" he said.

"Do you think we got the recipe right? Did we miss any important questions?"

"No," he said. "I think you got it perfect."

With that Jane put up another slide:

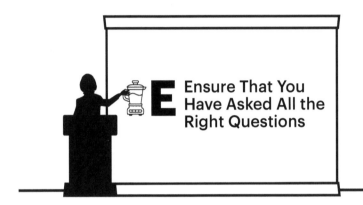

"Bob, have you had fun up here helping us to create this? Did you feel special being picked?" Jane asked again.

"Yes! It has been unexpected, and very fun!" Bob answered enthusiastically. "And I know my colleagues here are all very jealous." He followed up, earning jeers from his peers.

Jane up the next slide:

Jane turned to Bob and said, "Wonderful! I am so glad we delivered on all of our promises. Thank you, Bob. You can be seated again."

Bob, looking crestfallen and confused, just stood in place. "Don't I get my martini?" The crowd roared with laughter.

"Oh Bob," Jane said, her voice dripping with false sympathy. "I couldn't possibly ask you to take this. I'm just here to give you a great customer *experience*. I am not a salesperson." Laughter rolled through the audience again, especially at Bob's disappointed face.

"May I buy it from you? Please?"

"I don't know," Jane said hesitantly. "I don't want to be pushy and force you to buy it. After all, the only reason you came up on stage was to be my volunteer. You didn't come up here to *buy* anything. You already spent so much just coming to this conference. I wouldn't want to intrude by assuming you'd want to *buy* something."

The room laughed at this, but even more when Bob said, "But I really, really want it!"

As the room erupted in more laughter, Jane took Bob out of his misery by handing him the drink. He took a grateful sip, allowed a look of pleasure pass over him, and turned to salute Ken who nodded in acceptance.

Bob returned to his seat, and Ken moved offstage while Jane put up the last slide:

"Thank you, Bob. I think you all understand the point I am trying to make." She could see people nodding, including Bob, who was enjoying his martini to the chagrin and jealousy of those near him.

"I asked the question in the beginning about how many of your people are offended by the idea that they are salespeople. We all know that many professionals in the spa industry — in many industries, in fact — are afraid of the concept of sales, and they shy away from opportunities that can increase your revenue and future business," Jane continued. "They don't possess a *sales mindset*. But that doesn't mean that we can't help them to still deliver to our top line. We just need to know the right ways to approach them, train them, and continually develop them."

"Yesterday, I had the opportunity to visit a prominent spa here in Belfast. I won't tell you the name because, although most of what I am going to tell you is overwhelmingly positive, there is one potential landmine in front of this spa. If the esthetician who gave me my facial ever leaves, product sales will drop drastically."

She could see that she had everyone's attention still, even after speaking for nearly an hour. They could all imagine the scenario playing out in their own spas.

"Let me tell you how the spa rated in my BLEND strategy," Jane said, while slides popped up on the monitors.

"From the moment I entered the spa, I was greeted warmly by three staff members. Their method for welcoming me was inviting and made me feel like they had been waiting for me to arrive. They validated my choice of spa treatment and set positive expectations for the esthetician and the treatment.

"My provider greeted me in a unique and personal manner, making sure she knew my goals for the service. She offered me my choice of either being a quiet participant or to be actively involved in the process of my facial. Instead of going through the motions, she was fully present for me."

"I give them an A in this category."

"During my treatment, my esthetician made comments such as how my skin was reacting to the various products she was using, asked questions to ensure I was comfortable, and adapted to my responses. I have never before had someone tell me about the visual changes they could see on my face during a facial. I had always been simply the benefactor of the *feeling* of the facial. She recognized the visual and physical changes while I was experiencing the emotional ones."

"I give them an A in this category."

"Before, during, and after my treatment, my provider communicated in ways that let me feel I was in control of the service. Her questions were never an intrusion on my experience, especially since I validated my desire in the beginning to be an active participant."

"I give them an A in this category."

"By sitting down with me, face-to-face, prior to the appointment, to ask me what I wanted to achieve in the experience, I felt special. No one else who had been in the waiting room had received this type of personal attention. It was clear to me that she valued me and my patronage."

"I give them an C in this category."

At the crowd's confusion, Jane continued. "Although it was an exceptional experience for me," she said, generating eye contact with several people, "Note that I said 'No one else in the waiting room received this type of personal attention.' That means that this is not something that is being replicated throughout the company."

She could see that they understood this, and even if they didn't like it, they knew she was right.

"Finally, my provider gave me reasons to want to buy the products. By making comments about the products she used, referring back to when and how she used them, and pointing out the differences she noticed in my skin so that I could look for them too, she made me confident that those products would benefit me.

"I am happy to say that I bought several things, adding £100 pounds to my bill," Jane ended this with a smile while people clapped.

"But," Jane continued, quieting the group once again. "When I asked my provider how she became such a great salesperson, she looked at me with horror and said ... "

Jane paused for dramatic effect and then motioned the entire group to make the statement with her that she put up on the monitor.

"Yes, you all guessed it. This tells me that it is luck that this spa makes product sales. Luck that they have a great employee who believes in what she is using and genuinely believes that the client will benefit from it. Luck that she instinctively knows how to position herself, the product, and her company in a way that drives revenue."

"But," Jane continued, "their luck will run out if she ever does. Building a BLEND strategy takes vision, leadership, dedication, commitment, development, and training."

"I give them a C in this category as well. Simply because, this is luck. As with how she prepared me for my facial, her own efforts warrant an A. But as I said before, if she ever leaves, product sales go with her. She has not been trained and developed to do this. She does it because it is natural to her."

"It is not enough to *want* this for your business. You must be proactive in making this happen every day. Remember, customer service is how you are treated. Customer experience is how you *feel*. And people who *feel* valued will return time and time again. They will support your business. They will enhance your reputation. And they will refer their friends."

With that, Jane smiled, waved at the audience and said, "Thank you ladies and gentlemen. It has been a pleasure to speak with you today.

I will be around during the closing cocktail reception to answer any questions. And Bob," she said while he smiled up at her, "you owe me a cocktail!"

 Remember, customer service is how you are treated. Customer experience is how you *feel*.

Chapter 11

LEAVE-TAKINGS

Later that night, still feeling the energy of the day, Jane walked into Fred's for the last time. Her new friends were all in motion, and Ken's smile was genuine, as he indicated a seat that seemed to be waiting just for her.

"How did it go after I left?" Ken asked.

"It was fantastic! I had a tough time getting out of there as everyone had a comment or a question. I booked three more speaking engagements on the spot, and the association asked me to help them develop a comprehensive sales program they could offer to their members."

"That is great! Did you even get to enjoy a cocktail at the reception, or are you ready for one now?"

"Frankly, I could have had a cocktail, but I preferred to wait to have my favorite bartender make me one for my last night," Jane responded, making Ken smile even larger.

"Do you trust me?" He asked and winked.

"You know, I do! Bring it on."

A few minutes later Jane had another exquisite creation in front of her, this time a twist on a whiskey sour.

She took a sip, closed her eyes, and made noises that told Ken that she approved. When she opened them again, she found Jacqueline and Sandra near her, smiling as well.

"Thank you so much for inviting us today. It was fun to see how you took what we do here and applied it to another industry. We are going to be sorry to see you go! You are leaving us in the morning?" Sandra asked.

"Yes, I am. And I am sorry to leave. I will miss you all, and am so glad you let me share what you do with all of those people." Jane could feel the exhaustion portion of her post-presentation decompression, and she was getting a little emotional at the thought of leaving her new friends.

"We are going to miss you too!" Jacqueline said as Ken and Sandra nodded along.

"But this isn't goodbye," Sandra said. "If you are interested, that is."

Jane looked at her a little confused until Sandra continued.

"I've spoken to the CEO of the hotel, and we would like to invite you back when your book releases, all expenses on us. And we would like to purchase a copy of your book for each member of our staff."

Jane was floored. What a compliment! Before she could answer, Jacqueline piped in as well.

"And of course, you will have to bring your husband this time. Sandra's assistant will be reaching out to you soon so that she can keep track of your target date, and she will make arrangements for your flights and transportation."

"I would love to do that!" Jane exclaimed. "What an honor. I can't wait to come back."

Chapter 12

PARDON ME, BUT DO YOU HAVE ANY ... TABASCO?

As Jane got on the plane to leave Northern Ireland, she reflected on the past week. She couldn't believe all that she had learned on a trip where she went to teach others. *But I guess that's what it's all about,* she thought. *If you keep your eyes and ears open, and you're fully paying attention to what is going on around you, you can find unusual things you weren't expecting.*

She settled into her seat, smiling because on this flight, after so many years of flying, she would cross the million-mile mark with this airline.

She liked and traveled on other airlines, but she was a believer in loyalty when it was deserved. And sometimes, it just felt like home.[21]

Travelling in business-class for work, was a luxury Jane never took for granted. She relished every overseas flight, especially as an adventure, from the first welcoming glass of champagne to great meals, and the little details in between. But much like the question she had posed to Sandra and Jacqueline and kept contemplating, she wondered again if you could become immune to consistently good service.

She watched the flight crew as they welcomed passengers aboard more closely than usual, trying to keep her new heightened awareness of excellence. The teams on overseas flights were usually top-notch, but she watched with them now with fresh eyes. An older gentleman with a cane and suitcase was quickly helped by one attendant who offered to carry his bag and help him get settled.

A couple with two young children and a newborn quickly found help. The father and two children were introduced to the pilots, while another attendant helped the mother find their seats and settle in.

Another traveler in business-class boarded, then became frantic when she couldn't find her phone. An attendant called the gate agent who assured them the phone was found in the jetway. Crisis averted and stress reduced.

The flight attendants balanced both their position responsibilities with a calm and attentive focus on passengers. Thinking back to her BLEND principles, she found them all in practice with this team.

Once they were in the air, the flight attendants began to offer drinks. Jane couldn't help but overhear the request of the man across the aisle from her as he ordered a Bloody Mary.

"Any chance that you have spicy Bloody Mary mix?" he asked.

"Our mix isn't spicy," she said. "But I may be able to come up with a few things to help make it spicier."

"No worries," he said. "I was just curious. I can drink it regardless. I just enjoy spicy ones better."

She smiled as she walked away to prepare his drink, and Jane was curious. She rarely ordered a Bloody Mary on flights because the mix was so bland.

A few minutes later, the flight attendant returned with his drink and an assortment of a few other things: a tiny bottle of Tabasco sauce, a cup with wedges of lemon and lime, a small clear packet of what appeared to be olives, and a set of salt and pepper shakers.

Delivering this spread, she said, "I can't dig up any horseradish, Worcestershire sauce, or a celery stick, but hopefully these things will get you closer to what will make a great Bloody Mary."

The gentleman laughed out loud, almost with a boyish sense of glee. "This is fantastic!" he said, smiling. "I never thought of this as an option. I seem to always have these little bottles of Tabasco left over from meals. Why haven't I ever thrown one in my briefcase?"

She smiled and said, "Well if I may suggest, put them in a sandwich bag along with your leftover salt and pepper shakers today and keep them in your briefcase for future Bloody Mary emergencies." As she walked away, Jane caught the man's eye, and he saw her smiling as much as he was.

"Can you believe that?" he said.

"That was great!" replied Jane. "It is the second phenomenal cocktail and customer experience I've had this week."

"Really?" he asked, looking confused.

"Yep. I had one on my first night in Belfast. It so great that I've already begun working on the concept for my next book."

"You're a writer?"

"Yes. A writer and speaker. I speak and write about potential — leadership potential, sales potential, and the potential of exceptional customer experiences. What I just witnessed needs to be documented." She pulled the notebook from her bag.

"Tell me more," he said, making Jane laugh. She pulled out a copy of her book, also from her bag, making him laugh now as he read the title.

"Now, if only I could predict the stock market as well!" He said, smiling and chuckling. "But seriously, I'd like to know more about what you do. My name is Barry and I am the CEO of a training and professional development app. It's called TrainRS."

"You have got to be kidding me," said Jane. "This is too much of a coincidence." They both had a good laugh when she told him about her recent encounters with The Prenton.

"That is so funny," he said. "I was in Belfast meeting with the CEO of the hotel talking about how we can take the success at The Prenton and pull it through their other locations around the globe."

"I think that is a great idea, Barry. I would like to stay in touch with you as well. I have a number of clients who could definitely benefit from this resource."

"I agree," said Barry, fishing in his briefcase for a business card. Please email me next week and let's schedule a call. I think there are a number of ways we can work together."

They chatted for a while longer as Jane told him about Fred's, the opportunity to be a part of their training, and her intentions for her next book.

"I think I'm going to call it *Sales Mixology*," she said, saying it out loud for the first time to test how it flowed.

"Interesting title. But do you think people might not understand that, and maybe think it's a book about cocktails?"

"Possibly, but it seems so right. I like the fact it will make people stop to think, and to begin to look at a variety of experiences with the same expectation as an amazing night out."

"I can see that," said Barry. "Jane, I am so very glad we met."

"I am as well," said Jane. She was overwhelmed by all the positive events of the last week. And this one just seemed a perfect conclusion to an exceptional trip.

Hours later, following a delicious meal and succumbing to dessert, Jane finally snuggled into her pillow and comforter, leaning back with her headphones on while the sounds of snoring and people quietly visiting faded around her.

She smiled as she relaxed, grateful that she was able to *BLEND* personal and professional experiences into something delicious.

EPILOGUE

Full Circle – Jane's Perspective

As Jane walked into the convention center, she was excited to see Maria. They had exchanged texts in the past few days and planned to have dinner together tonight after the conference ended for the day. She couldn't wait to hear what Maria thought of her new shoes. Neon green with purple sequins. They were a gift from Stephen and Jack.

She was also mentally checking off the list of things she had to do before her flight next week back to Belfast. She was so excited to see the whole team there again. They were closing Fred's for the night for an invitation-only book signing event. Jane could hardly wait to get there, this time with her husband in tow.

She was so deep in thought that she almost ran into a woman who had bent down to retrieve something on the ground and smiled as she realized the woman was Maria.

"I was hoping I'd find you before the day got started," Maria said, smiling and giving Jane a big hug.

"Me too! I've got about ten minutes before I have to check in with the speaker's lounge. You look great. How is everything?"

"Jane, I can't believe how great this year has been, and that it's been a year since I met you. The company is doing fantastic.

"We are blowing our revenue budget completely out of the water, and my reorganization has been seamless. My people are achieving heights they never knew possible, all because of something that woke me up last year at this time. I cannot tell you how thankful I am that I met you!"

Jane smiled at the praise but, in her usual manner, deferred the compliment. "Maria, I just gave you a tool. You chose to use it. I have something for you," Jane said as she pulled something from her bag.

It was a hard copy of *Sales Mixology* signed just for Maria.

"Jane! You got it finished!"

"Yep. I didn't have it done in time for submission for this year's conference, but I'm certainly going to plug it! I want you to have the first official copy. I think you will enjoy it!"

Maria laughed as she took the book.

"Really, Jane? Do you think I'll like it? Tell Me More!"

The women laughed as they walked towards the speakers' lounge.

"It certainly sounds like it was an adventure writing this book," Maria said.

"It was. I have spoken on leadership for so long, and it allowed me to look at things in a new light."

"How so?" asked Maria.

"Well, you know I work with all kinds of companies. I realized that every company, every organization, every business has something to sell, and a customer to sell it to."

Maria nodded her understanding. It was a statement she whole-heartedly agreed with even though she often found people who were resistant to the concept of sales. She added her thoughts.

"I know what you mean. You may make have a product, provide a service, or promote a mission, but you have to have people 'buy' it to be successful. Any non-profit with a mission to help others can't be successful unless people believe in and support the mission. They buy it by buying-in."

"Exactly!" Jane said. "And selling your idea or product or service or mission is only the first step. To maintain success, you have to take good care of the 'customer' who is buying it. If you don't, they won't come back." Maria nodded her agreement.

"You know Maria, of all the things I learned this last year, I truly see how leadership bears the responsibility to create positive and productive workplaces. I've seen it in action and, thanks to my time with The Prenton, I am making those changes in other companies. It's like helping the business, and all its people, to reach their full and destined potential. Shocking, isn't it?"[22]

THE BLEND WORKBOOK

I hope that this book has adequately illustrated how the customer experience can be one of the greatest assets to your business's success. Customer experiences should not happen by accident, however, or you will never enjoy *consistent* customer loyalty. People have more choices now than ever before for how and where they shop, and they are letting either their experience, the price, or both dictate their buying decisions.

People are still willing to pay more for certain goods and services, but only if the overall experience is phenomenal and consistent. If either of those two ingredients is absent, people will choose price and convenience almost every time.

Whether you sell a good, a service, or a mission, the BLEND principles — as outlined in this book and presented here in a practical workbook — should be a litmus test of your focus on and delivery of exceptional customer experience. I urge you to complete the following activities as they relate to your business, attempting to look through the eyes of your customers. Even better, ask your customers how they would rate you on these areas.

Don't be afraid of the responses. If you are off the mark, it is better to know now and adjust than it is to continue on a path that won't build lasting success. If you are already meeting all of these objectives, congratulations! Now think about how you want to ensure this in the future. Complacency is your enemy.

I believe that training is the critical, and often missing, ingredient. Many companies provide lackluster training, and, even if they do have a training plan, it is often only offered to new hires. Even worse than dull training is on-the-job training. On-the-job training means, "We don't have a training plan. We depend on current staff to pass along their knowledge, right or wrong, to new employees who will hopefully succeed through luck."

 On-the-job training means, "We don't have a training plan. We depend on current staff to pass along their knowledge, right or wrong, to new employees who will hopefully succeed through luck."

Although you might find the training program at The Prenton Hotel to be unattainable (see Endnotes on page 183), I have used variations of these trainings for many years with great success. The story allowed me to bring various methods together to highlight in one condensed package. It also allows me to illustrate some of the ways my company is working with our clients to develop comprehensive training programs, as you observe in the examples from The Prenton. Developing exceptional content and working with great technology business partners like ShareLook, my company is changing the landscape of company training programs. After all, comprehensive and on-going training should be a cornerstone in every company.

If you would like to know more about how to create genuinely impactful training in your company, we are here to help. Reach out to us at Info@ShockYourPotential.com. My team is dedicated to helping you to create a *Positive and Productive Workplace.*

BLEND Principles

B – Be Immediately and Fully Present

L – Listen with Your Ears AND Your Eyes

E – Ensure That You Have Asked All the Right Questions

N – Never Let Your Customer Feel like a Number

D – Deliver an Exceptional Customer Experience
(Being Mindful of Financial Return)

B – Be Immediately and Fully Present

What does it mean in your business to be *immediately and fully present* to your customer and your company? In a retail store, this is obvious. If you have walked into a store and found the salesperson on their phone, barely able to pull themselves away long enough to say, "Let me know if I can help you with anything," you know they are not immediately and fully present.

If you have walked into a business of any kind and stood in front of the receptionist or clerk, who clearly knows you are there but fails to acknowledge you for several seconds or minutes, this is a culture that accepts less than immediately and fully present behavior. If even one person on your team operates this way, you have made this behavior acceptable.

We assume that when we hire people that they will instinctively know how we want them to act, and interact, with the customer. But unless we have trained them well in the beginning, and provide ongoing training, including recognition for those who achieve and exceed expectations, then we operate by hope instead of strategy.

Complete this exercise:

1. What should it look like for our employees to be immediately and fully present to our customers?

    _____

    _____

    _____

2. Who on my team operates this way right now, without fail?

_____

_____

_____

3. Who on my team does not operate this way?

_____

_____

_____

4. What can I do to gain buy-in with my team and make this
   a priority?

_____

_____

_____

L – Listen with Your Ears AND Your Eyes

When you have employees who are immediately and fully present, they are always on the lookout. They are usually aware of what is going on around them and are actively looking for ways to operate in support of the mission.

The server in a restaurant who only has one table, but who will run food or bus tables for his/her colleagues to ensure the restaurant operates smoothly, is acutely aware of what is important. The person in a store that opens up a new cash register when too many people are in line is paying attention.

Some of these actions are mandated by company policy, and yet many people do it simply because they are aware. They put themselves into the shoes of the customer and/or their colleague, and want to ease stress and strain.

I use the term "listen" for both visual and auditory cues because both are equally important, and both tell a story of a customer's satisfaction. But remember, this book isn't just about service. It is about experience. The best people will strive to give the best experiences.

The best companies ensure that their teams know *how* to give the best experiences.

Customer service is how you are *treated*. Customer experience is how you *feel*.

Complete this exercise:

1. What do my customers want in an exceptional experience with us?

   _____

   _____

   _____

2. What kinds of visual and verbal cues do my customers give us
   when they *are* satisfied?

   _____

   _____

   _____

3. What kinds of visual and verbal cues do my customers give us
   when they *are not* satisfied?

   _____

   _____

   _____

4. Who on my team recognizes visual and verbal cues consistently?

   _____

   _____

   _____

5. Who on my team *does not* recognize visual and verbal cues consistently?

_____

_____

_____

6. What can I do to train my team to excel in this skill?

_____

_____

_____

E – Ensure That You Have Asked All the Right Questions

Salespeople are often trained to *sell*. In many points in my career, I was given a sales script, and just as many times I created and taught salespeople to use scripts. But what seemed to elude most of my salespeople was the art of using a script as a guide rather than seeing them as lines to be memorized.

Memorization is critical in the beginning of a new sales strategy because it ensures that you know all the essential steps by memory. But if you deliver a script by rote, you will sound rote.

The art of asking questions does many things. It allows you to learn more about what the customer *wants* rather than the salesperson trying to reach their own goals independently. It also allows the customer to begin to buy-in along the way, thus leading to a more natural, and more relaxed, sale.

If you ask *all* of the right questions, an *appropriate* sale will be the direct result at the proper time.

 If you ask *all* of the right questions, an *appropriate* sale will be the direct result at the proper time.

Note that I don't say that a *sale* will be the direct result. Sometimes a financial transaction is not appropriate. Sometimes your product, service, or mission is not what the customer needs. When that is the case, you did not lose a sale. You helped the customer better understand their own need.

When the product, service, or mission is what the customer needs, you can determine whether they are willing to pay your price. If they are not, you still did not lose a sale. You learned more of what the market, and that customer, will bear. But if they are not willing to pay your price because you didn't ask the right questions through the process, then you did lose an opportunity.

Finally, when the product, service, or mission is what the customer needs AND they are willing to pay the price, they will buy from you when the time is right for them. Hopefully, that will be now, but if not, you should understand how to best continue the relationship with them until they are ready to complete the purchase.

Too many salespeople assume if the customer doesn't buy now, the sale is either lost or the person will return on their own when they are ready. But the salesperson who asks all the right questions will know the best way to keep connected to that customer. These savvy salespeople take what they've learned from their interactions and devise an on-going communication plan with the customer and are there when the customer is ready to commit.

Complete this exercise:

1. What are the best questions we can ask our customers at every stage of the sales process?

   _____

   _____

   _____

2. What questions are salespeople afraid to ask the customer?

_____

_____

_____

3. What is the danger in *not* asking these questions?

_____

_____

_____

4. Who on my team is good at asking the right questions, and enough of them?

_____

_____

_____

5. Who on my team is more likely to either use a script too closely or to go rogue because they *know* how to do it their way?

_____

_____

_____

6. What can I do to train my team to help them master this skill?

_____

_____

_____

N – Never Let Your Customer Feel Like a Number

People who shop online for price and convenience still want a good experience, but they are often willing to forgo a *great* experience. They know they are just one of many customers.

But if we are trying to create and maintain *exceptional* experiences, the customer does not want to feel like one in a million. They want to be seen, heard, and cared about. The heart of this story shows the many ways we can ensure that the customer feels unique, and that their business is wanted and respected.

It is easy to get so caught up in business that we forget the customer. But there are simple ways to keep your employees focused in the right direction.

Complete this exercise:

1. What interactions could lead our customers to feel like they are a number?

   _____

   _____

   _____

2. What are the best solutions we could/should/do implement to ensure that they do not feel like a number?

   _____

   _____

   _____

3. Which member of my team receives the most positive customer comments? Why is that, and how are we recognizing them?

_____

_____

_____

4. What can I do to train my team to help them master this skill?

_____

_____

_____

D – Deliver an Exceptional Customer Experience (Being Mindful of Financial Return)

Do your employees respect and protect the financial assets of your company? Do they have a genuine emotional investment in the fiscal health of your company? Whether you answered yes, or no, how do you know you are correct? If you answered, "I don't know," why not? More importantly, how can you ensure that they do care?

This book was designed to illustrate that when your employees are thoroughly hired, trained, developed and retained, they are more likely to have the best financial interests of the company in mind in the execution of their responsibilities.

This concept is more than whether an employee uses the company printer for personal documents or takes home office supplies. This is about the decisions they make that affect the financial viability of the company, in big ways, and small.

In contrast, I also want to show that managers are often be conflicted about how to allocate resources in situations where allowing more leeway will increase financial returns. When the characters discuss people coming on shift in Fred's to accommodate a large group, this highlights how sometimes we can be so blinded by what we think we *must* do that we don't always think about what we *should* do.

The story allows me to illustrate this conflict in a very tangible way, yet it is not a simple matter, either. A company must trust that their employees will make good decisions on behalf of the company and customer. The employee must also feel safe enough to make decisions that impact both the customer and the company in positive ways.

Complete this exercise:

1. What leeway does your team have now to make decisions for the customer that impacts the financial health of the company?

   _____

   _____

   _____

2. What methods are some of your team using to impact the customer experience that don't provide an immediate benefit to or negatively impact the financial health of the company?

   _____

   _____

   _____

3. Do you trust your team enough to make decisions like the concepts illustrated in the story that could have a positive impact on the financial health of the company? Why or why not?

   _____

   _____

   _____

4. What can you do to train and develop your team to make decisions in this manner?

   _____

   _____

   _____

THE STORY BEHIND THE BOOK

This book is a vehicle for my own tried, tested, and proven sales and customer experience strategies, and it provides an opportunity for us to discuss the changing customer experience landscape. Please note that I use the term "customer experience" rather than "customer service" deliberately. Customer service is how you are treated. Customer experience is how you feel.

People use the terms interchangeably, but they are vastly different strategies. Customer service should bring to mind things like politeness and courtesy. Customer experiences, however, are about ensuring that the customer is fully engaged with you, your product, and your brand.

I developed the concept for *Sales Mixology* quite a few years ago with a blog called A Cocktail a Day where I highlighted excellent cocktails served with an exceptional experience. It wasn't good enough for the cocktail to be delicious; anyone can make a tasty cocktail. I had to feel that there was a more in-depth design where the bar, restaurant, or bartender focused on making the customer feel welcome and making her want to return.

None of the people or places in this book are representative of the content of the stories. Instead, each is used to illustrate my message that positive and professional people deliver excellent customer experiences.

In the following pages, I highlight some places and people that were inspirations for components of this story, as well as some of the blog posts I wrote about them. I am a firm believer in praising the best experiences. I want great people and companies to continue to be recognized and celebrated.

 I am a firm believer in praising the best experiences. I want great people and companies to continue to be recognized and celebrated.

The best businesses know how to attract, hire, train, and retain exceptional employees. At the end of this book, I highlight several companies that I found filled with the highest percentage of these types of employees.

There are always exceptions to the rule, even in great companies, but the following businesses have consistently proven to be staffed by predominantly positive and professional people who make me want to return as a customer over and over.

END NOTES – INSPIRATION

Throughout this book, you have seen superscripted numbers, 1 through 22, associated with key stories, companies, places, brands, people, or experiences. Those numbers bring you here, for more insight and flavor. Some of these stories were originally shared in my ongoing social media series, *Thoughts from the Coffee Table*.

1

The Merchant Hotel – Belfast, Northern Ireland

The Prenton Hotel in this book is modeled after The Merchant Hotel in Belfast, Northern Ireland (www.TheMerchantHotel.com).

I have been fortunate to travel in both Ireland and Northern Ireland in connection with speaking engagements. The team who hired me to speak insisted on putting my husband and me up for a couple of nights at The Merchant Hotel.

This hotel is one of the most beautiful hotels I have ever stayed at, and the overall customer experience was exquisite. The story about the people at The Prenton, the training program and the management processes are my original designs; they do not reflect anything about how this hotel operates. However, I assume that their training and development program is superb, given the overall experience and well-deserved reputation of the hotel.

Other hotels have also shown me great examples of excellence in service, especially Marriott and Hilton properties.

Thoughts from the Coffee Table:
I became a Marriott Rewards member about 25 years ago, on my first business trip. Happy Golden Anniversary to me!

My husband and I tell people we have a mixed marriage. I am Marriott Lifetime Platinum and he is Hilton Diamond. Not lifetime though. I lord that over him whenever possible.

This week I met Tonda, a dynamo in the concierge lounge at the Renaissance Cleveland Hotel. A team member

Happy Golden Anniversary!

for 26 years, Tonda is the embodiment of everything wonderful about this brand. Happy Belated Golden Anniversary, Tonda!

Her smile is giant; her laugh is genuine; she knows guests personally; she greets everyone as they arrive and hates to see them leave; she clearly loves her job; and she definitely loves the company that she works for.

How do you hire for this kind of character? How can we find a Tonda for every critical customer-facing position?

Over two days, interactions with every team member in this hotel have been outstanding. Despite Tonda's innate fabulousness, there is clearly a culture here of finding, and retaining, great people.

This type of professionalism mixed with pure personality is business magic, the level we should each strive to achieve. And I found it here in beautiful downtown Cleveland.

Thoughts from the Coffee Table: When I go to visit my son and grandchildren, I often spend the last night at the Seattle Airport Marriott. After all, who wants to make a 7:00 a.m. flight while trying not to wake toddlers at 4:00 a.m.? Frankly, who wants to wake up at 4:00 when you can sleep until 5:00?

And who wouldn't want to actually SLEEP the night before a cross-country flight?

For the Love of Marriott

As I checked in, I shared stories from my week, and commented that after I returned my rental car, I was looking forward to a nice glass of wine and a big comfy bed without a squirming 3 ½-year-old in it.

When I returned to my room, this was waiting for me.

I just stood there and looked for a moment. And frankly, I might have teared up just a bit. I was exhausted ...

Yes, I am Lifetime Platinum with Marriott. Yes, I have stayed at this hotel numerous times. But the value of this gift, to me, is well beyond all of that. Katie truly listened to me, heard what I didn't say, and took it upon herself to do this thing for me. Just for me.

I knew I couldn't drink more than a glass that night so I wrapped it up in my suitcase, and went down to the lobby bar to buy a glass — to give back.

And tonight, now that I am home and relaxed, I am going to open this up, and toast Katie and Marriott.

Thoughts from the Coffee Table: I have been reflecting on all the little moments of excellence I have observed this week at the JW Marriott San Antonio. When I ask for directions, people come from behind their desks. In the gift shop, a lovely woman worked the upsell with a grandmotherly smile. Housekeeping leaves us sweet notes.

Then we met Fernando.

Fernando at Cibolo Moon
JW Marriott San Antonio

Fernando was our server last night, professional and engaging, exuding confidence that made you trust him. He worked the table, never intruding but never leaving us wanting for anything.

But what made him extra special was his passion for tequila.

Cibolo Moon has a crazy selection of tequila, including many that they infuse on-site. Fernando is considered a tequila sommelier, and his knowledge is impressive! Most of us enjoyed a spicy margarita named the Nando after Fernando, with muddled jalapeño and a chili salt rim. Just to be sure I liked it, I think I should go back for one more.

Fernando taught us about plant varieties, harvest and preparation. He not only knows his stuff, he loves what he knows. He is living proof positive that if you love what you do, you will never work a day in your life.

And if you go to see him, have his margarita. And the chicken fried steak. Definitely the chicken fried steak ...

Thoughts from the Coffee Table:
I am participating in a large conference at the JW Marriott San Antonio. The fact that we are here is lucky enough as we were supposed to be in Naples, Florida and that Marriott property was severely damaged by Hurricane Irma.

The property is beautiful. Countless team members have proven a dedication to exceptional service, including the shoeshine man, who is a miracle worker! And despite being off-season, there are multiple activities throughout the resort like 7:00 a.m. yoga, which I slept through again today ...

Lantana Spa
JW Marriott San Antonio

As I perfect my presentation on Shock the Upsell, my premise was proven this week in the Lantana Spa. Ask for me to buy one more thing, and I will. Make it genuine and compelling, and I will say yes. Make it important to me and prove that you care about me as much as the sale, and I walk away very happy. The spa team did that, and more.

I realize I am a somewhat unusual consumer, but at our core, we all want the same things. We want to be respected. We want to be cared about. We want positive experiences.

And some days we want a bath bomb. And lotion that smells like marshmallows.

Thoughts from the Coffee Table: The Essex House is an amazing hotel in New York City overlooking Central Park. I have been blessed to stay there for business a few times. Every time I walk in, I am greeted by the most amazing floral displays. They are true works of art.

I have never eaten in the restaurant, Southgate. We always have someplace to be, and there is also a stupidly wonderful pizza place out back with butter garlic knots. I digress.

**JW Marriott Essex House
New York City**

I was not staying in New York City this time, but decided to have lunch because I was walking by. Quiet on a sunny Tuesday, I took a place at the bar to be able to work, look out, and relax.

The wild king salmon was amazing, the Barton & Guestier Chablis lovely, but the true gem was Bappy. Yes, the bartender's name was Bappy.

Each person working in that restaurant gave me a warm smile and openly welcomed me. There was a vibe that was simply lovely. It could be easy to be stuffy given the address of this hotel. Last time we stayed, guests from the United Nations filled the hotel. I was a bit out of place.

True excellence requires genuine people, comfortable and confident in themselves. This team has that in spades.

Next time, I will suggest we eat at Southgate, after we have a butter garlic knots appetizer, of course.

Thoughts from the Coffee Table:
This stunning piece of art sits tucked around a quiet corner in the DoubleTree by Hilton in Santiago-Vitacura, Chile, no artist listed. In fact, of all the sculpture I found in Santiago, none listed the artist. But the impact this one, in particular, had on me, was significant.

Leadership Art
DoubleTree by Hilton
Santiago-Vitacura, Chile

At first glance you might assume that this is about people at the top standing on the shoulders of others, holding them back so that they may rise to the top.

When you look closely, you will see that everyone is connected. Everyone is supporting and lifting another person while they climb.

At the very bottom, you find several people who were clearly once a part of the base who are now being lifted.

I am a firm believer that leadership means raising those around you to a higher level.

As I get back into reality after 16 days in Peru and Chile, I am so thankful for each experience. Today, reach down for someone else and give them strength and stability to continue their climb.

Thoughts from the Coffee Table: OK, call me a sucker. I probably am in many ways. But the small gestures during travel make me smile.

Hilton – Lima, Peru

Friday we set off on an adventure that is part pleasure and part work, flying to Lima, Peru. Our flights were good and relatively short (only six hours from Atlanta) and we enjoyed only a one-hour time change. Nonetheless, arriving in a new country at midnight can be daunting and exhausting.

Our first few nights have been at the Hilton on points, and even though I should expect it by now, the sight of a welcome snack in room fills me with childish glee.

This plate was especially delicious, because although we are seasoned travelers, there is nothing like being "welcomed" with food. Many other great experiences have followed, but this one effort truly set the stage.

2

Northern Ireland

If you have not traveled to Northern Ireland, I would highly recommend it. (www.VisitBelfast.com)

On our third trip to the island of Ireland, we took several days to explore Northern Ireland and thoroughly enjoyed every minute. This book highlights a couple of our adventures in Belfast such as the Black Taxi tour and the Titanic Museum, but we also fell in love with Bushmills and the Giants Causeway (www.Ireland.com/en-us/Amazing-Places/Giants-Causeway).

I initially intended for Jane to visit Bushmills, taking a whiskey tour at the Bushmills Distillery (www.Bushmills.com) where my husband and I received an incredible education from our 22-year-old tour guide. I also wanted Jane to stay at The Bushmills Inn (www.BushmillsInn.com).

Both of these experiences, even during a freezing and wet January, are forever stamped into our hearts. For you Game of Thrones fans, we also visited a few of the sites highlighted in key episodes.

Ultimately, I left out Jane's trip to Bushmills because, although I have great stories and memories, it was unnecessary. Perhaps she will get another chance in a future book.

3

Fred's Jazz & Cocktail Lounge

Fred's is based on Berts Jazz Bar located in The Merchant Hotel. (www.TheMerchantHotel.com/Bars-Restaurants/Berts-Jazz-Bar)

The Merchant Hotel has several amazing venues for cocktails, including the aptly named The Cocktail Bar (www.TheMerchantHotel.com/Bars-Restaurants/The-Cocktail-Bar). Cocktails are not just on the menu at this hotel. They ARE the menu.

I had never seen a cocktail bar with this level of attention to perfect detail. We were mesmerized by the creative process and thrilled with the results.

4

P.F. Chang's – Hartsfield-Jackson Atlanta International Airport – Terminal A

If I have a layover of any amount of time in Atlanta, I always head to the P.F. Chang's. Yes, I am a fan of the Chicken Lettuce Wraps, but I am even more a fan of the consistently high level of positive service. This team always delivers an excellent experience for weary travelers. The first time I noticed the note cards used to remember my name and drink I was blown away. This is such a simple thing to do, yet it makes the entire experience more personal.

5

The Onion Bar & Grill – Spokane, Washington

I am a firm believer that everyone should be required to wait tables in their career. You learn a different level of hustle and must fight to create positive experiences for customers, often in very stressful situations. In my early 20s, I waited tables at The Onion Bar & Grill in Spokane, Washington. The training required me to work in the bar, as a food runner, a busser, and a greeter (hostess). There were also times when those were my shifts, depending on the need of the restaurant.

We wore buttons that said "No Problem," and this concept has stuck with me for my entire career. We were taught to say "No Problem" to customer wishes that would enhance their experience.

If someone wanted a baked potato as their side, we said "No Problem" even though we didn't have them on the menu. I had the authority to take cash out of the till to give to a food runner who then called in an order to our competition in the shopping complex, which sold baked potatoes. The receipt went into the till, I never charged the customer more, and they got their baked potato.

It was a hard concept to get used to in the beginning. I was always afraid I would get in trouble. But I soon learned that putting the customer first was never punished.

Two examples stick out most in my mind. The first was when I had a group of men as a business lunch in my section. When I got to the last man, I asked: "What would you like for lunch?" He responded with "I really want a Big Mac. But my wife has me on this damn diet. So I'll have the Rhonda Stir-Fry."

You guessed it. I sent someone out right away for a Big Mac. I brought him his stir-fry first, along with the other meals. And about five minutes in, I presented him with the Big Mac. He was ecstatic! He was the star of the table; he got a great laugh, ate a few bites, and left a unusually generous tip. I know he left with a wonderful memory.

The other memory is from a man who called himself "The Garbage Man." He wasn't a Sanitation Engineer, but he was a regular. He would come in about every other week, order the special burger of the day, and ask for you to "garbage it up."

We all knew The Garbage Man, and the moment he walked in the door, the kitchen got excited and began getting creative. "Garbage it up" meant that he wanted anything and everything on that burger, and it was entirely up to the kitchen. They tried weird combinations, they added peanut butter, they made statement pieces. We probably spent $20 in ingredients on his burger that he bought for $6.99. But it was always worth it.

The Garbage man always brought in at least two people, often more. He relished in his unique fame. He was a walking "No Problem" billboard. I also believe we created new burger creations because of him. It was a symbiotic relationship.

I don't know if The Onion still operates this way today, but it played a formative role in my views of sales and customer experiences.

6

E. Schweitzer, Master Sommelier, 2003-2011 – The Grand Hotel – Mackinac Island, Michigan

I was invited to conduct training many years ago with a group that was meeting at The Grand Hotel on Mackinac Island, between the Lower and Upper Peninsulas of Michigan. The island is a stunning walk back in time, with no motorized vehicles allowed and a place to buy, and make fudge on every corner. Seriously.

The Grand Hotel is a simply stunning locale with a penchant for stories about being haunted. I must admit that there were noises in the halls at night that I couldn't account for,

We had both a wine tasting with our group as well as a multiple course meal with wine pairing per course. Master Sommelier, E. Schweitzer, oversaw both events. I was fascinated by the dedication to achieve that status, impressed with her knowledge and love of wine, and, after making a joke during the tasting about boxed wine, I was educated on the merits of boxed wine.

The character Olivia is based loosely on E. Schweitzer. It was a great opportunity for me to pair (pun intended) the technical components of wine with the sales strategies for an exceptional customer experience.

www.GrandHotel.com

7

Terra Blanca Winery – Benton City, Washington

Terra Blanca Winery is one of my happy places. I was fortunate to find it many years ago, when their tasting room was still a mobile home on top of the hill, overlooking the Yakima River.

Today, Terra Blanca boasts a spectacular tasting room, has a restaurant, and a sunset view that you have to experience to believe. The staff has always been amazing. I was a wine club member for many years until I moved to Philadelphia, where, at the time, you could not receive wine club shipments. Thankfully that law has changed!

I held several business events at Terra Blanca in a previous professional life. One of the greatest I can remember ended with the sunset, a glass of their exquisite Onyx, and me singing jazz songs with the small band I hired for the event. Some places are simply magical, and this is one.

I used Terra Blanca as my muse for Olivia's journey to Katherine's family vineyard, but the rest of the story is my original creation.

www.TerraBlanca.com

8

Stephen Leddy and Ken Vinney – Hidden Hearing, Ireland

I have two dear friends who are responsible for my experiences in Northern, Ireland. They also might be responsible for some fun adventures in other parts of the world, but those things will have to come out in another book altogether. "The Irish Boys," as I fondly refer to them, would prefer if no one ever uses the term "awesome" ever again. Instead, they would like us to use their catch response of "Amazeballs." I couldn't let this book come to print without thanking them for their friendship, and their never-ending supply of energy, laughter, and love for my husband and me.

9

Horizon Hospitality

In researching data on turnover rates and costs for employees in the hospitality industry, I came across the following article by Horizon Hospitality and asked their permission to reference it. Written by Leigh Ann Teubert, Managing Partner, Client Relations, Leigh Ann makes some great points about the real costs of turnovers.

In my experience running enormous sales organizations, I can confidently say, a two-fold process of hiring practices and employee training and development can make or break a company. I wanted to give a soft reference to the data Leigh Ann quotes to make the same point she does. Do it right the first time, do it right through the life-cycle of the employee, and any added costs for these two efforts will be more than made up against the costs for high turnover.

Read the article: www.HorizonHospitality.com/2013/01/29/ What-Is-Turnover-Costing-Your-Restaurant/ Learn more about them: www.HorizonHospitality.com

10

CVS Pharmacy – Fairmount Neighborhood, Philadelphia

Jane's view references precisely how I feel about the CVS in my neighborhood. There is actually another CVS now a few blocks in the other direction that makes me feel exactly the same way.

Thoughts from the Coffee Table: I do not believe in trophies for all, even though I still have a 7th place ribbon for the 200-meter backstroke when I was 10. It is baby blue.

There is a CVS that I shop at frequently. It is close, has an awesome selection of ice cream, padded envelopes and a great rotating cereal sale. I used to hate the receipt as long as I am tall, but now I feel like I'm at a slot machine waiting for my winnings. Michael loves a coupon!

As I walked out yesterday, I wondered why I had not written about this store yet. Then I realized something.

I always write about "shockingly" great experiences.

At this CVS, I have consistency.

Every team member is nice, cheerful, and welcoming, without fail. Everything I need is always available. Every line moves at the right speed, or else a team member intercepts.

I have never had a negative experience in this store. Ever.

So, to the CVS in Fairmount in Philly, I want you to know that you are doing a great job! And I apologize that I haven't recognized you yet for what you are: Consistent in representing your company, and yourselves, with positivity and professionalism!

I'll bring by the trophy later ...

11

ShareLook - Live Assessments

I have been privileged to be a part of the launch team for ShareLook, and innovative training and professional development tool. There are many facets to this app. The one that is most exciting to me is the ability to take a Mystery Shopping experience and turn it into something truly dynamic and progressive for any company. There is the opportunity for interaction, live feedback, and a replay option for review later. If you would like to know more, please reach out to my team at Info@ShockYourPotential.com.

12

Belfast Black Taxi Tours

Although I had heard of Black Taxi Tours before in other cities, I can say, without a doubt, that it was one of the best experiences I have ever had. My husband and I saw parts of the city that would have never been accessible to us, and we felt honored to have been given such open and honest descriptions of life in Belfast.

To learn more: www.BlackTaxiTours.com

13

LUSH Handmade Cosmetics and The Body Shop

I first went into a LUSH store several years ago just to see what it was about. I had heard a little about it and was curious. Now I am a life-long fan. Here are a couple of *Thoughts from the Coffee Table* blog articles I have written about them.

I had heard about LUSH from several people but had never gone into a store until 2017. My first visit was in the Center City, Philadelphia, Pennsylvania, location. I was blown away.

Upon arrival, the aroma is the first thing that hits your senses. The person who greeted me at the door was well beyond the "Hi there. How can I help you?" personality. I later learned her name was Tally. Her demeanor was infectious, and she seemed thrilled I walked through the door.

When she asked what she could help me find, I told her that I had never visited LUSH before and just wanted to see what they had. She said, "Let me get Stephanie to show you around!" and was off before I could object.

Stephanie was a spectacular example of true love of the products and her company, and a wealth of knowledge. She knew every ingredient of every product and talked about how they were made, all while engaging me in a series of questions much akin to the *Tell Me More* strategy that is the core of my first book *Tell Me More — How to Ask the Right Questions and Get the Most Out of Your Employees.* The strategy works just as well from a sales perspective, and Stephanie used it perfectly. I soon had a beautiful collection of things to try from bath bombs to bubble bars to a face cleanser.

Before I left, I asked Stephanie about the training program at LUSH, and she fessed up to being the store manager. She spoke about how every employee was trained on the products the same way.

LUSH has been a part of my world ever since. I have visited their stores all over the country. Of particular note are the stores in New York City on 34th Street and the store in the Tacoma Mall in Tacoma, Washington. I even visited a location in a mall in Santiago, Chile where the young lady working that day, fortunately, spoke enough English to counter my poor Spanish.

This company is no joke. The people that work there want to work there. They believe in the products and the mission, and they come to work because they want to.

LUSH Loot

Thoughts from the Coffee Table: There is a slight possibility that I am addicted to this company. I'd like to say I can quit anytime, but that would be a lie. LUSH, I can't quit you!

Yesterday I treated a friend to a spa treatment that, for me, had been life changing. OK, I realize that sounds melodramatic, but when I had the Synesthesia treatment last summer, I was overwhelmed by the beauty of the connection between massage for the body and balm for the soul.

While there, I had to restock my bubble bar collection and pick up one or two (maybe four) impulse purchases. I also had the opportunity to watch this team in action.

I did sales leadership training with this team last spring, and I adore them. But I also watch them with a critical eye.

As with any retail sales training I do, I discuss how no customer is never "just looking." Every time I say that, people jump out of their chairs to tell me I am wrong. I love it! Then we talk about how to counteract.

This team takes the concept seriously and is a joy to watch in action.

Maximizing sales requires you to *listen* to a customer in a different way. Great products are important, but an engaged and committed team is the secret sauce. In my view, LUSH has the right recipe for both!

Thoughts from The Coffee Table: By now my love of LUSH products and people is not a secret. This company constantly amazes me.

If you have a store in your city, go watch the flow of people as they shop. They are like kids in a candy store, as am I.

I have also been fortunate to make genuine connections with many on the team, and yesterday I got to meet Mama Roxy!

Mama Roxy – LUSH

If you know her given name, you are in the inner circle. But her role as Mama Roxy is legendary. Her background and life story is just as epic.

I feel blessed that I got to spend a few hours with this amazing woman yesterday, becoming even more confident in the quality of people who choose to be part of the LUSH life.

Mama Roxy, you rock! (See there? I made a funny!)

By the way, I bought a bubble bar for my grandbabies and we filled the tub last night with "lushious" colors and smells. The giggles and genuinely hard laughter was making my 14-month-old granddaughter snort. It was priceless. What more could anyone want ...

LUSH Spa – Perspective
in Philadelphia

Thoughts from the Coffee Table:
As a thank you for my leadership training with the LUSH team, I was treated to a spa treatment. I had no idea what to expect from something called Synesthesia. It has taken me all week to describe this experience, and I fear I still will not do it justice.

I have had great spa experiences before, but never anything like what I can only describe as life altering. I know that sounds a bit dramatic, which is part of the challenge I have had in writing about it. At its core, this is an 80-minute massage, but it is so very much more. Asked to pick a focus for my treatment from a list of emotional states, I chose Perspective.

This is a massage that incorporates all senses, and the particular focus on sound took me on a journey. Simply stated, this was transformative.

There are only two LUSH spas in North America — Philadelphia and New York. The artistry of their spa concept, the attention to details I've never seen employed in this fashion, is a gift in itself. I can't believe that this gem has been in my own backyard without knowing about it!

Finally, Adrienne Williams, my therapist, was a complete joy. I gained Perspective this week, and I have her to thank for it!

Thoughts from the Coffee Table:
What role do your senses play in an amazing customer experience? What does the smell of a freshly baked chocolate cupcake, merged with the cold application to a warm face, play in your belief in a product? I may also have a secret desire to eat this facemask out of the jar while standing at the fridge …

Sometimes I think my senses rule me, but that isn't a bad thing.

**Cookies or
Cupcakes Anyone?**

Once upon a time, I was a marketing director for nursing homes. We had the oldest buildings in town, and the competition was building sparkling new places all around us. One of my receptionists told me that she toured one of the new places. I panicked because I thought she would rather work there than in our old, but loveable, buildings.

Instead she said, "That place smelled like popcorn and happiness. Our buildings smell like sick people and Pine-Sol." I was devastated.

But her condemnation also came with a solution. "I think we should bake cookies near my desk. Then when family comes to visit or tour, it smells like home."

Soon a cookie oven sat at every front desk.

A simple solution to a problem of emotion and senses. And a reminder to always look, smell and feel through the eyes of the customer.

Just don't eat the facemask.

The Body Shop

It's too bad that my first experience in The Body Shop, more than 25 years ago, ended in a missed opportunity because I could have been a customer for much longer than I have.

At that time, the company had a loyalty program that cost (if I remember correctly) $25 annually. Of course, there were many ways to recoup that investment, but the person who talked me into saying yes didn't give me enough information, and I didn't understand the charge. I never renewed and didn't go back to the store.

Flash forward ten years. I received a gift basket for a birthday filled with all sorts of goodies, including Body Butter that changed my life.

I am not kidding in any way when I say that I use The Body Shop Body Butter every single day, without fail, from head to toe. Well, from neck to toe.

What I find when I enter one of their stores, anywhere in the country, are happy and personable sales professionals. I have never seen one that did not impress me in some way.

While shopping at the Frisco, Texas Stonebriar Centre store many years ago, the salesperson asked me if I had ever tried the shaving cream. As it was in the men's section, I assured her I had not. She told me it was life-changing and sent me home with a sample. I was back the next day and have not been without that product ever since.

The Center City Philadelphia location is my go-to spot; the team there always a joy. They closed the doors a while back for a remodel, which made me crazy. I almost ran out!

Most impressive, however, was a message I received one day from the manager of the Northshore Mall location in Peabody, Massachusetts, just outside of Boston. Rachael had been following me for some time on LinkedIn and told me the next time I was in the Boston area, I should visit their store.

A few months later, I was in Boston for business and made a special trip to see Rachael and her team. I have to admit, I felt like a rock star. I was pampered, had my makeup done, and the entire staff had read my book, *Tell Me More*.

Thoughts from the Coffee Table: This week I was invited to be pampered by the team at The Body Shop in the Northshore Mall, Peabody, Massachusetts. Rachael, the store manager, has been following my posts and honored me with the invitation.

As #SecretShopperMichael, I write about great leadership, sales and customer service experiences when I am neither expected nor known. Being invited, I expected to see greatness. But what I experienced was much more.

**The Body Shop
Peabody, Massachusetts**

Rachael, Gisbel, and Felicia pampered me, no doubt. I felt like a rock star!

But it was the way they treated every other customer that really spoke to me.

In particular, a group of special needs adults and their caregivers were having an outing at the mall. Many stores might wish a group like this would move on, but not Rachael and her team.

The group was joyously welcomed to smell, feel, and see the products in action.

No purchases were made, and at times the caregivers seemed nervous as to not overstay the welcome. But everyone in the group had enormous smiles.

Service means more than sales. And yet service, given freely and without judgement, will always reap rewards.

As I left, the team thanked me for visiting them. But the thanks belong solely to me. I was transformed that day by their humanity.

14

#SecretShopperMichael

I began using #SecretShopperMichael a few years ago to highlight overwhelmingly positive customer experiences. I only highlight excellent examples; never negative ones. It is my firm belief that we should praise in public and correct in private. I carry special business cards with me at all times to leave with people who have impressed me. The card invites them to follow me and lets them know that they might be mentioned in a future *Thoughts from the Coffee Table* blog post.

15

The Titanic Museum

My time at the Titanic Museum is one that I will never forget. It is impossible to express the attention paid to the tiniest details in each room on the ship. The story is an excellent reminder to me that, although attention to the fine details is critical, we should never overlook the most significant dangers we face. www. TitanicPigeonForge.com

16

ShareLook

ShareLook has a live feed feature allowing leaders with admin access to broadcast to all employees at any time. The ideal use of this feature is for regularly scheduled meetings to replace conference calls or to share critical and immediate information. Participants can submit questions or feedback via a comment section. If you would like to know more, please reach out to my team at Info@ ShockYourPotential.com.

17

ShareLook

ShareLook is an e-learning solution, allowing businesses to create digital content for a variety of reasons. At Shock Your Potential, we are using ShareLook to build a library of business resources for our clients who access the materials via a subscription model. We also help our clients create and implement training programs they can use via ShareLook or the app-portal of their choice. If you would like to know more, please reach out to my team at Info@ ShockYourPotential.com.

18

Shock Your Potential

As the CPO (Chief Potential Officer) of Shock Your Potential, I have first-hand experience in creating and implementing training programs that are described here and ascribed to Jacqueline. The programs can help ensure new hires are fully integrated, weed out inappropriate hires before the 90-day probation period is over, and create a culture of on-going learning and professional development.

The "train the trainer" model has proven itself to be ineffective. At Shock Your Potential, we go straight to the employee and provide them the training they need, creating the vehicle for the leadership team to monitor and adapt training, as needed.

19

Omni La Costa Resort & Spa (Carlsbad) – Near San Diego, California

The introduction to the spa and the spa staff at the reception desk comes directly from a wonderful spa experience I had at the Omni La Costa Resort & Spa near San Diego. The team there was fantastic in a multitude of ways. www.OmniHotels.com/Hotels/San-Diego-La-Costa/Spa

20

Eviama Life Spa – Philadelphia, Pennsylvania

The character Mary-Kate came from my treatment provider at the Eviama Life spa in Philadelphia. She sat with me prior to the facial, establishing rapport. Although Mary-Kate uses some techniques that are unique to her character, the sense of welcome and inclusion was the heart of this great experience. www.Eviama.com

21

Delta Airlines

Delta Airlines holds a special place in my heart, most importantly, because I met my husband on a Delta flight, and a few years later, I proposed to him on a Delta flight. I am still cranky with him that he refused to get married on a Delta flight. I was pretty sure we might have gotten a free honeymoon out of it.

I didn't start as a Delta customer. I began as a Northwest Airlines customer and was not sure what to expect from Delta when the two airlines merged many years ago.

My husband just achieved million-mile status with Delta, and as I write this, I have just more than 100,000 miles to go for that status as well. We are loyal.

That doesn't mean that there aren't blips along the way or the occasional cranky flight attendant, but for the vast majority of my years with Delta, I have seen excellence in a multitude of forms.

Thoughts from the (Sea-Tac Delta Sky Club on A) Coffee Table: I have been a Delta Sky Club member for as long as I can remember. Until last July when I let my membership lapse, due to changing travel patterns. Today my hubby got me in, and I don't want to leave.

His plane is heading to Salt Lake City; mine is delayed beyond belief due to storms. I decided to fly tomorrow instead, yet here I sit.

Flight Delays? Who Cares?

The staff here is amazing. The woman who rebooked my flights was a joy, even when she had to give me the bad news that I could be stuck here, or stuck in Detroit, likely without a hotel.

The bartender gave the most professional advice on my hubby's beer choice. He could have the free one included in his membership or spend $4 for an upgrade. She gave him the description of their comparative hops value. Fantastic!

Finally, the onsite Asanda Spa Lounge seems like one of the best business decisions ever. I could use 5,000 of my 300,000 Delta Air Lines miles for a facial! Imagine the impact on the bottom line for a few massages instead of more free flights?

I watch people go by, most business travelers, and some clearly agitated by flight delays. Sure, I had to reschedule six appointments for tomorrow. But the examples of excellence right now are worth the layover.

Thoughts from the Coffee Table:
Because I fly Delta more than any other airline, it comes as no surprise that I write about them more often than others. I am constantly impressed by the quality of their teams and their commitment to deliver exceptional customer experiences.

While in Santiago, Chile, we witnessed many Delta crewmembers in a more relaxed environ-

Sherlock is His Name!

ment because they stayed in our same hotel. One with serious opera pipes even serenaded us!

This is Sherlock. Yep! Sherlock Martin Wilson!

He couldn't wait to get to my seat, knowing my last name is Sherlock. Before reaching me, I watched him interact with each person in front of me. He was charming and joyous, exuding energy I found infectious.

The entire crew on our Santiago, Chile, to Atlanta flight was great, but Sherlock made my day. The power of a smile and a laugh, and the ability to take a job seriously while not taking yourself too seriously, is something to treasure. Until we meet again, Sherlock!

Thoughts from the Coffee Table:
Yesterday in Santiago Chile,
I found an example of excellence
in service that I did not expect.

I am primarily a Delta customer,
although I have had exceptional
experiences on other airlines. The
hotel we are staying at in Santiago
has been filled each morning with
Delta flight crews at breakfast.
But this woman was something
special. She was running around
the breakfast room with what
I believe was a bag of the Biscoff
cookies, making sure each member of the DoubleTree staff got one.

Carlas

As she made her way to people, she left them each with a giant smile.
The cookies were not the reason. She SAW these people and appreciated them. She has been to this hotel before, and the team loves her.
The cookies were not the reason. She did more for the Delta brand
than any commercial. And still, the cookies were not the reason.

I asked her name and if I could take her picture. She radiates joy.
Although I asked twice to make sure I got it correct, I believe her
name is Carlas. I hope I didn't screw that up.

When we fly home tomorrow night, I pray she is on my flight. I hope
to see her again and witness her spread even more joy.

Thoughts from the Coffee Table: How can I have fallen so far so
fast? It seems like just yesterday I was Diamond with Delta; this year
just lowly Gold. I walk past those with their first-class upgrades with
barely checked envy.

OK, I am a little melodramatic.

I felt like I'd lost something until I flew from Minneapolis-St. Paul International Airport to Sea-Tacoma International Airport. The caliber of the cabin crew was out of this world!

**Move Over United!
Delta Flies the Friendly Skies!**

I was nervous, heading on this trip to take care of my grandchildren. I was preparing for 10 days, many of them all by myself, with a 3 ½-year-old and 1½-year-old while my son got some much-needed rest and relaxation.

OK, I wasn't nervous. I was terrified!

While chatting with Joseph, he learned of the reason for my trip, and soon his three colleagues did as well, thanks to him. April, Amanda, and Jordan all checked-in on me multiple times assuring me I would do great and could handle two tiny people on my own. And my coffee cup never ran dry.

The human connection was what I craved that morning. The sense that others cared for and supported me. Knowing these people saw me as a person, not as a number.

And now that I am home (I survived!), I reflect.

I didn't need an upgrade to feel special. Joseph, Amanda, April, and Jordan proved it personally.

One cup of coffee at a time ...

Thoughts from the Coffee Table: OK, it is 4:45 a.m. in Seattle, and I realize that cookies are not an acceptable breakfast. But how do I say no to gingerbread cookies?

Travel is hard, but the little things can make all the difference: a superbly pleasant shuttle driver from the Seattle Airport Marriott; smiling and happy TSA agents; a Delta team member undaunted by the line of people waiting for the Sky Club on A to open at 4:45 a.m., and then making it faster by checking people in with a handheld device.

**Gingersnaps for Breakfast?
Yes Please!**

And gingerbread cookies!

Simple kindnesses, small gestures, and surprising details move in the world like a pulse.

I sometimes wonder if these people know how much they impact weary travelers like me and like you, that they are sometimes lifeblood and sometimes life support, just by the smallest of details.

I begin a long journey home. I leave behind two beautiful grandchildren and a son who makes me so proud. My heart is breaking a bit.

As I dive into this cookie it makes me think of sweet little hands that would devour this treat and cover Grandma with those sticky happy fingers.

A thought that makes me smile. Thanks to an airline that gave me a cookie.

22

More Remarkable Brands Worth Mentioning

Finally, I'd like to highlight a few other businesses whose dedication to excellence in service have impressed me enough to write about them, at least once, in my blog:

Thoughts from the Coffee Table: I love things that sparkle. From my very first job in a high-end jewelry store where we sold tiny Swarovski crystal figurines, the company has fascinated me.

That Swarovski Sparkle

I went on Friday to purchase some earrings. Of course, I wanted everything is the Atelier Collection by Mary Katrantzou. I need to find the right reasons my husband needs to buy them for me! Or in case Swarovski is reading this, I would be happy to accept them as a gift.

Never hurts to try ...

What I also love about Swarovski is their talented and attentive staff. These folks know their product and breathe customer service.

I worked with Robert this time at the Walnut Street location in Philadelphia. He is an impeccable dresser with a fabulous sense of humor, a perfect mix of professionalism and humanity.

Since I was also finally replacing two damaged rings that I wear as wedding bands, he heard my confession. I damaged them and lost crystals because I cleaned them in the dishwasher — few times.

Poor guy. He was trying so hard not to laugh at me.

People like Robert evolve a brand. They make you want to shop in a store where you can see and touch and dream.

And they make me want to continue a relationship with a company that truly sparkles.

Thoughts from the Coffee Table:
At 16, I worked as a gift wrapper in a jewelry store. Hired only for the holidays, I was selling on the floor within weeks. I showed  a passion for learning, watched how my colleagues dressed, and sold a diamond engagement ring on my first day!

I was fascinated by the Swarovski figurines. On slow days you would find me looking at those miniature works of art. My husband bought my first Swarovski earrings, and I was hooked! When we got married, I purchased two bands to go with my ring. I stare at them as much as I did in that glass case decades ago.

Last week in New York City, I met Leslie at the flagship store on 7th Avenue and 34th Street. I have lost a crystal in each band, and as Leslie listened to my story and I explained how I cleaned all of my rings in the dishwasher, she very politely did NOT call me an idiot.

Offering to send them in, I said I was planning to buy two new bands. Leslie went through EVERY box in her store looking for my size, to no avail. Because I live in Philadelphia, she spent time ensuring my store had them, refusing to let me leave without a plan.

The wonder and magic I felt at 16 looking at those crystals stay true today through the products and service I experience in these stores. Now the real question is, what ELSE will I buy?

Thoughts from the Coffee Table:
Thanks to a post by a LinkedIn connection referencing new products at The Bath & Body Works, I had no choice but to go in search of these items (pictured here) in my local Center City Philadelphia Bath & Body Works. In my continued research on the customer experience, this time, I was shopping for products only.

**Bath & Body Works
Philadelphia, PA,
Center City**

As I entered the store, for the first time in at least five years, I was surprised by Aaron, who jumped up from behind the front display.

Of the three employees in the store, I had interactions with two, Aaron, and a young lady. Both were exceptional in their greeting to me and in engaging me about the products. But Aaron's energy and personality are infectious. I watched him interact with every customer and each of his colleagues, and I couldn't help but smile.

Frankly, listening to his story about using the shapeable soap when it came out was the best part! These products look fun, and I suppose I am going to have to send shapeable soap to my grandchildren, but not until I've played with it first …

Thoughts from the Coffee Table: Chris was the name of my first ever boyfriend in 7th grade. He rode a BMX bike, had long hair, and wore Vans. I believe he became a philosophy professor.

Vans for Life!

None of that has anything to do with my purchase of Vans yesterday, but it makes me laugh. I was looking for a great pair of walking shoes. The staff of the Center City Philadelphia store impressed me with their genuine welcome. They cared I came in!

The relaxed, yet focused sales environment caught my attention. This team was unique. I never got the name of the man who helped me, but I assume his name is Charlie based on my receipt.

Three things that made him stand out:

1. He was a perfect mix of enthusiasm and professionalism.

2. He didn't fall for my "I'm just looking." He knew I came in for a reason and wanted to help.

3. His smooth attempt to upsell me to the invisible socks was perfection, even though I haven't yet bought them!

Finally, when I checked out at the register, the same comfortable attempt to upsell the socks was made, showing continuity and commitment.

This was a fantastic shopping experience, and reason enough for me to look for a second pair of Vans soon!

Thoughts from the Coffee Table: Last month, I bought my first pair of Vans. Now I *need* the baby blue Vans.

This week at the Northshore Mall in Peabody, Massachusetts, The Body Shop team invited other stores to meet me. I felt like a rock star!

**Vans and ASkate.org
Peabody, Massachusetts**

Bonnie and Lindsey, dynamic gals with a vision and a passion for making their store flourish, came from Vans. We discussed the balance of work and life, and their enthusiasm for their company was infectious.

They had read my earlier post on Vans and had a goodie bag for me with the invisible socks I referenced before but did not buy. And then they about fell over giggling, explaining they are called "no-show socks."

I learned about the A.skate Foundation, a nonprofit connecting autistic children with the world through skateboarding. Autism is near and dear to me, but it reminds me is that many companies that we love, support causes that we don't always see. When we slow down, ask, and engage, we can learn more about what they offer to the world beyond great products.

Do me a favor. Learn more about what your companies believe in, and support their causes that speak to you. For me, I am diving in, or rather skateboarding, to www.ASkate.org. Bring on the Band-Aids!

Thoughts from the Coffee Table:
Sales is art. You can be born with natural ability, inner confidence, or complete insanity, but you have to be able to be coached, learn from masters, and be willing to make a fool of yourself.

Some people struggle with the fool part, but not me. I make a fool of myself three times before breakfast.

TD Bank has been on my radar, but another story always seemed to jump ahead, until yesterday.

**TD Bank – 19th & Market Streets
Philadelphia, Pennsylvania**

A lady standing next to my teller asked me what kind of business I had. I said, "I'm a writer and speaker about leadership, sales, and customer experiences!" with a smile.

We had a fun talk about where I have spoken and my next book coming.

She asked me if I accepted credit cards, and I said yes, thinking this could be a sale! Whoop whoop!

She then asked if I used their credit card processing services because that was her job.

She was going for the sale!

I smiled and handed her my card and invited her to call me. She asked for the business, and I intend to give her a meeting.

I don't know if I'll switch, but I was so proud that she had the opportunity and took it. It takes guts. And moxie. And a willingness to be rejected.

And just like the ever-present lollipops, sometimes the rewards can be sweet.

Thoughts from the Coffee Table:
Monday Morning Mugs with Michael — OK, so this is not a mug. But after going into my neighborhood Starbucks on 20th and Callowhill Streets in Philadelphia, I had no choice.

Upon walking in the door, I was greeted with a bright smile from Claude (according to his name tag). I told Claude I wasn't sure what I wanted this morning and he dove right in with excitement about several new things. Something with mangos was his favorite! But he admitted, sadly, that there was no caffeine in it. It was lovely!

Starbucks
Philadelphia, Pennsylvania
Fairmount

When we agreed that I needed caffeine this morning, he suggested the sweet vanilla cream cold brew. I was hooked!

Every time I visit this store, I fabulous people greet me. Today was no different.

However, I noted a large number of orders for pickup, and it made me think. If you order to pick up, you don't get to meet Claude. You don't get the joy of having the barista call your name when your drink is done (which feels a little like winning the lottery to me). Why would you miss that?

Thoughts from the Coffee Table:
While in Tacoma taking care of my grandbabies, I frequently patronized the drive-through of the Starbucks on 23rd Street & Union Avenue.

Starbucks –
Tacoma, Washington

I was thinking about it this morning as I made my coffee at home. Now that I live on the East Coast (and don't own a car), I never find myself in the drive-up businesses that are the life-blood of the Pacific Northwest.

On the morning that I took this picture, I started ninth in line and had my coffee less than about four minutes. Pretty impressive!

What I love most about this location is the quality of the customer experience.

These busy drive-through baristas are chatty and happy and make you feel like you've had a valuable human connection when you pull away. I have never felt like a number, nor felt that they needed me to leave to keep the line moving.

It is so easy to be busy being busy, so easy to forget that volume doesn't have to mean speedy interactions. This team has crafted the art of conversation while crafting my Grande Vanilla Soy Latte, extra hot.

And now, it's time to get back to my sad coffee at home ... Or maybe time to get to my neighborhood Starbucks!

Good Morning America

Thoughts from the Coffee Table: Yesterday something amazing happened, leading to an important decision.

While in New York City, I was hoping to get into the *Good Morning America (GMA)* taping, something I've always wanted to do. I love *GMA*, watch it every day and even converted my husband into a *GMA* fan. In my vision exercises, I see myself being interviewed about my book by Robin Roberts, able to tell her how much I admire her sharing her personal battles with the world.

I only made it to the waitlist.

While watching *GMA* from my hotel room, I sent Robin a tweet. To my shock, she responded! After a few interchanges, I received notice that she followed me. With over 1.1 million people following her and only following about 1,500, she chose me!

Six months ago, I began using social media to build my brand, trying every day to stay true to my mission of finding excellence. To be chosen this way by someone I admire so much was humbling. But the story doesn't end there.

She invited me to be in the *GMA* audience next week and has agreed to read my book. She doesn't know me. She owes me nothing. But her kindness has proven what I already knew. She is awesome! So now the real challenge: what shoes to wear?

Thoughts from the Coffee Table: Have you ever been to the orchestra? I spent six years of my life playing the violin. I had a purple velvet jacket that my mother made me wear so she could find me in the crowd at concerts. I spent years in therapy over that jacket, although today I would like to have it back.

This morning I had a new experience in the audience at *Good Morning America*. Much like my friend Joey Kola for Rachael Ray, Tom Kelly is the warm up guy for *GMA*. He is amazing!

Good Morning America
Tom Kelly – The Warm Up Guy

Warming up an audience is no easy feat. You need to give direction, raise energy levels, and make people feel at ease. You must add humor, mix in personal touches to engage individuals, and get a sense of who's in the room.

A live show must be a little like trying to conduct Spring Allegro not knowing what instruments are in the pit.

Tom was Conductor Extraordinaire through this chaos. In particular, he found a young girl in the audience, from Oklahoma nonetheless, and before we knew it, she was up with a mic (before the show) singing. The gift Tom gave this girl and her mother had us all in tears with giant smiles.

When you stop being star-struck and watch the dance of the production team, it is clear that this is art. I wonder if Tom owns a purple jacket ...

Thoughts from the Coffee Table: There may not be enough words in my brain to express my joy at being in the *GMA* studio this morning, and meeting Robin Roberts.

I learned late last night that there would be no audience today, but that I was still invited as a VIP to sit in the

**Good Morning America
Robin Roberts**

main studio through the entire show. I arrived early and a lovely woman immediately greeted me. Watching the personable, professional, and focused crew was fascinating. It takes many talented people working in tandem to pull off a two-hour live show, and they were terrific.

I feel so blessed to have met Robin, see her in action, and have her take my book. In person, she is who I imagined: professional, lovely to the people around her, and a genuinely joyful soul.

Now ... time for a nap!

Thoughts from the Coffee Table: Do my nails look like that?

I was out for dinner, and everyone at the table finished their meal, except me. Jack's Firehouse is a favorite and, although I didn't know the name of our server, he knew mine. That always surprises me.

When he came to clear dishes, he asked if I wanted a box, and I replied, "Yes. It looks like I am the only loser who didn't clear her plate."

He returned with our complimentary freshly baked chocolate chip pecan cookies and my leftovers, and we all commented on how great of a server he was.

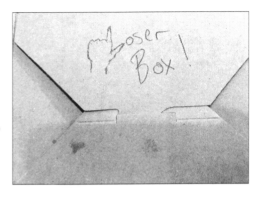

The next day, I opened the bag to enjoy my leftovers at lunch, and couldn't believe my eyes when I saw the box. I laughed out loud.

**Jack's Firehouse – Philadelphia
Take it Like a Loser**

What makes a memorable dining customer experience? Certainly, all the things you'd expect like great food, excellent service, and great environment.

But the small signs of personalities, a sense of humor, and, in this case, artistic abilities, made a lasting impression. And a reminder why this place is one of our favorites.

They constantly surprise me with little things, yet always deliver on the core. I suppose that's why it is the place we take all guests to on their first night in town. I know our guests will be treated well and enjoy it.

Like losers ...

Thoughts from the Coffee Table: The Logan Hotel sits in a perfect spot in Philadelphia. It was formerly a Four Seasons and we were saddened when it closed a couple of years ago to become The Logan.

We weren't saddened because we loved the other hotel. We were concerned that we would no longer see one of our favorite people.

There is a man who was a bellman at the Four Seasons, and this man could make the day of every person in Philly. When he is outside and not with a guest, he waves, smiles, and shouts good morning to every passerby.

Because I walk my husband to work on mornings when I am home,

**Anthony at the Logan Hotel
Philadelphia, Pennsylvania**

I realized we began to only walk in a path that took us by the hotel. When The Logan opened, we were thrilled that not only was this man still working there but that he had been promoted!

For the past several months we have had to walk a different path due to other city construction, but yesterday we walked by and were delighted to be greeted by him! It was like coming home.

I was going to get his name again this morning, but he was busy making someone else's day. I guess I have to share him with the rest of the world ...

Thoughts from the Coffee Table: Meet Diego Valle. Diego was our guide, and became our friend, during our trip through the Cusco region and glorious days at Machu Picchu.

If you follow my posts, you know I focus on excellence in customer service, the quality of sales processes, and of course, leadership. Diego encompasses all those traits, and more, all the while making you feel valued and welcomed.

Diego's knowledge of Peruvian history was beyond expectation. He watched to ensure that we enjoyed the trip at every point, especially conscious of the effects of very high altitudes. Diego is a freelance guide, which makes me so doubly glad that he was assigned to our group through Belmond.

Diego Tours Peru! – Diego Valle

Our travel companion set this itinerary with the help of TenDot Travel, a fantastic incentive travel company.

The worst part of our trip was saying goodbye to Diego. We hope to see him again! And if you plan to Vivian, Peru, let me know so I can connect you with him!

Thoughts from the Coffee Table: After leaving Machu Picchu, we traveled back to Cusco, Peru, via an extraordinary train. The Belmond Hiram Bingham train was named after the man who discovered Machu Picchu. I use the term "discovered" loosely because the locals already knew about it.

Belmond Tours

This three-hour trip is on a fabulously elegant train, with features that take you back in time, and a four-course meal with crisp white linens. The level of service on this trip was mind-blowing, but what made the event for me was Gorki, both server and bartender.

Once the train departs and you have made your meal selection, you are invited to visit the bar car where there is a fantastic band and an open bar. Gorki was our server, and I watched him quietly refreshing drinks, ensuring no snack dish went more than half empty, and offering to take pictures while still balancing his silver serving tray in one hand.

After dinner, we found Gorki behind the bar, pouring us a lovely whiskey and making us feel like we were in his home.

As we pulled into the station and realized our trip had to end, he asked me to complete a survey of our experience if we found it acceptable. Hmm ... let me think about that for a moment ...

Thoughts from the Coffee Table: As I witnessed the sunrise over Machu Picchu yesterday morning, I found myself overwhelmed with gratitude. I have a wonderful life filled with many blessings.

This trip is slightly more than half over, and the number of stories and examples I have of excellence in customer service are astounding. The level of hospitality and genuine joy and care of travelers by the Peruvian people has far exceeded all of my expectations.

Tomorrow morning, I believe I will tell the tale of Gorki, a bartender extraordinaire on the Belmond Hiram Bingham train. Look for the glass of whiskey to highlight the tale. Or maybe one of the hundreds of others.

This morning, I am still thankful and intend to drink up my whole last day in Peru with the wide eyes of a child.

Thoughts from the Coffee Table: A beautiful woman knelt in one of the gardens in our hotel, all day yesterday. She quietly wove, smiling and concentrating, with a table close by filled with the fruits of her labor.

We walked by her, and I snuck a quick picture when we headed out for our last tours of Cusco, and I wondered if she would be there when we returned.

During our final full day in Peru, we drank in all that we could of this culture and did a little bit of shopping. I had fun trying to barter for a necklace with people who don't barter, and we both walked away happy. But when we came back to find this woman still kneeling and weaving, and we took the time to see and touch what she made, there was no bartering. I would have paid almost any amount to purchase a hat for me and a scarf for my husband. We are leaving with gifts of her talents.

I leave Peru today, blessed to bring this culture with me.

ACKNOWLEDGMENTS

I love writing. I always have. I wrote poetry as a child. I wrote my first novel in my mid-20s. Don't worry. You haven't missed it. I keep it locked away, so no one discovers how bad it was.

I once had someone mock me, saying that I wasn't an author because I used a small publishing company for my first book, which I have since released in a 2nd edition. That makes me laugh.

I am an author because I write, because I am inquisitive, and because I have passion, dedication, and a desire for teaching others through the written, and spoken, word.

I am an author because people buy my books, because they read my blog, and because they ask me to write for their publications.

I am an author because I write.

Writing is a glorious method of creative expression, and writing can be a maddening exercise in self-doubt. I could edit my material until the end of time, but at some point, you have to put it out there and let the world take it: warts and all.

When I found my publishing partner in *Silver Tree Publishing*, I found a home with creative and crazy people just like me. They help me bring out my vision even brighter than I could imagine, and they are always there on the days I want to bury my head in the sand. I have felt lifted, supported, cheered, and understood.

Whatever the world mocks you for, remember others believe in and support you. Find the tribe whose members surround you with love, encouragement, energy, and editing. Those who truly love us can also speak the truth to us. And when we love ourselves, we can hear it.

ABOUT THE
AUTHOR

Michael Sherlock is a leadership and
sales expert, known globally for her
ability to present serious business
concepts in a uniquely memorable
way. Her credentials include serving
as Vice President of Sales for two
different global medical device
companies and navigating both of
those sales organizations through
profound structural and operational
changes. In these positions, she
was responsible for hundreds of
employees and hundreds of millions
of dollars.

Today Michael serves as the Chief Potential Officer of Shock Your
Potential, her Philadelphia-based training organization. She and
her team provide corporations and business leaders with action-
able strategies of leadership, employee development, customer

experience, and sales transformation. Additionally, Michael was invited to serve as the Chief Commercial Officer for ShareLook, an app-based learning management system. Her role encompasses the creation and implementation of the global sales strategy.

Michael holds a BA in Education from Eastern Washington University and has delivered keynote presentations and trainings internationally. Outside her professional life, Michael is an avid urban gardener, a passionate home chef, and a struggling student in the art of meditation. She enjoys traveling to countries around the world, and immersing herself in new experiences, languages and cultures.

Sales Mixology is the second book in the *Shock Your Potential Series.*

KEEP IN TOUCH!

🌐 **Learn more about *Sales Mixology*, and quickly connect to Michael Sherlock on her website:**

ShockYourPotential.com

🎙️ **Listen to the podcast:**

ShockYourPotentialPodcast.com

✉️ **Send an email:**

Michael@ShockYourPotential.com

@ **Find, follow, and share on social media:**

- 📘 Facebook.com/MichaelSherlockSpeaks/
- 🐦 Twitter.com/MichaelSSpeaks
- 📷 Instagram.com/ShockYourPotential
  and Instagram.com/SalesMixology
- 💼 LinkedIn.com/MichaelASherlock

DON'T GO JUST YET!

Get Started Reading Book 3 of the "Shock Your Potential" Book Series!

Shock Your Potential: Igniting Profit at the Positive Intersection of Leadership, Sales, and the Customer Experience

Shock Your Potential continues the learning adventures started in *Tell Me More* and *Sales Mixology*. Visit www.ShockYourPotential.com to find out how to buy your copies of Michael Sherlock's other books!

SHOCK YOUR POTENTIAL

By Michael Sherlock

PROLOGUE:
You Like Me! You Really Like Me!

To: Belfast Journal of Business Subscriber

From: Belfast Journal of Business Editor-in-Chief Owen Smithson

Re: Time for the Top 40-Under-40 Nomination Process

Dear Belfast Journal of Business Subscriber:

As you know, each Spring we ask you to help us compile our list of the Top 40-Under-40 Professionals in Belfast. The nomination process is simple, but we need your help. If you know an outstanding professional who is making a positive impact on our business community, we want to know about them.

Please follow the link at the bottom of this email with instructions on the submission process. *Deadline for submissions is June 30.*

Sincerely,

Owen Smithson, Editor in Chief

To: Owen Smithson

From: Sandra Merkle

Re: Top 40-Under-40 Nomination Form

Dear Barry:

I am excited to nominate Jacqueline Murphy, the Director of Training here at The Prenton Hotel. I am confident that once you read my submission, you will be as impressed with her contributions as I am, and as our company is. She is already on the radar of our CEO and Board of Directors. I imagine it won't be long before she is given greater opportunities within our global company.

In addition to the submission form, I am attaching letters of recommendation from five of Jacqueline's colleagues as well as our company CEO and the Chairman of the Board.

If you have any questions, please don't hesitate to call.

Sincerely,

Sandra Merkle, General Manager, The Prenton Hotel

Nominee Name:	Jacqueline Murphy
Position:	Director of Training
Company Name:	The Prenton Hotel
Nominated by:	Sandra Merkle
Position:	General Manager
Company Name:	The Prenton Hotel

Why should we consider this nominee for the Top 40 Under 40 Professionals list?

Jacqueline has been with The Prenton Hotel for more than three years, and her hiring, training, and continual development programs have revolutionized how we do business. She takes a multidisciplinary approach to learning, ensuring that our training reaches a variety of learning styles. She also works diligently to ensure that each of our employees is fully and continuously trained.

Jacqueline believes that great companies begin with great people. But great people are the by-product of systematic hiring protocols and on-going training. She believes that we should have the right people in the right positions doing the right things.

When she came on board and presented her hiring and training platform to me, she had already vetted the process in a smaller hotel venue with great success. We needed substantial operational changes at The Prenton Hotel, and I knew her strategy had merit. Now, more than three years later, I know we made the right decision.

I am confident that the following nomination form will clearly and distinctly set her apart from her competition.

CHAPTER ONE:
40-Under-40

Jacqueline sat at her desk in her office on the 4th floor of The Prenton Hotel in Belfast, Northern Ireland. The late September day was bright and sunny, like most of the fall had been thus far. It had been an unusually warm summer, and the autumn seemed to hold lingering bright sun and unseasonable warmth. She idly wondered if she had time to take a walk outside before the staff meeting later that afternoon.

The night prior had been filled with fun and excitement. They held a large private event in Fred's Jazz & Cocktail Lounge to celebrate the launch of Jane Smith's newest book, *Sales Mixology — Why the Most Potent Sales and Customer Experiences Follow a Recipe for Success.*

Jacqueline couldn't help but smile, thinking of her friend. It had been nearly a year since the two had met while Jane was in Belfast speaking at a conference. While staying at The Prenton, Jane had developed the material for her second book. She gained much of her inspiration from the comprehensive training program that Jacqueline had designed for the hotel.

Jacqueline had been the Director of Training for the hotel now for slightly more than three years, and during that time, the hotel increased its profitability and efficiency at a rapid pace. Working hand-in-hand with Sandra, the General Manager, they had also decreased turnover substantially, increased staff satisfaction, and improved guest ratings exponentially.

We've created a positive and productive workplace here, mused Jacqueline, smiling at the line Sandra used as her personal motto. *I wonder how we top this.*

As if by magic answer to her question, the phone rang.

"This is Jaqueline," she said into the phone.

"Hello, Jacqueline," said a man's voice on the other line. "My name is Owen Smithson with the *Belfast Journal*."

Jacqueline assumed that he was calling to sell her a subscription, and mentally berated herself for not letting an unknown number go to voicemail.

"Hello, Owen . How many I help you?"

"Well, Jacqueline, I am calling to congratulate you for being chosen as one of our Top 40-Under-40 Professionals in Belfast for the year."

"What?" she asked, confusion in her voice. That wasn't what she was expecting to hear.

Owen laughed and said, "I get that response a lot. It's always a shock coming out of the blue. You are not only one of our top 40-under-40; you are our number one pick. I am calling to schedule a time to interview you and do a photoshoot."

Jacqueline was even more confused and dumfounded by now. "Owen, you have me at a loss for words, and that is not an easy thing to achieve!" she said, now laughing a bit at herself.

"How was I chosen?" she asked; still a bit confused by the call and wondering if it was a joke.

"Great question, Jacqueline. Each year we poll our subscribers and ask them to nominate people they think are worthy of making the list. A committee, which includes the editor, the mayor and several other members of our board, reviews each nomination and narrows them down to the top 40. Then from that 40, we rank them in terms of their impact on our city."

"I can't even imagine who would nominate me," Jacqueline said. Right then, Sandra, the General Manager for the hotel, poked her head in the door with a slight grin on her face. As Jacqueline waved her in, Sandra sat in one of the chairs and Jacqueline put Owen on speakerphone.

"Wait, Owen. Before you answer that, I think I may know now who nominated me." Sandra gave an offhand shrug of her shoulders, and her grin got even bigger.

"Well," Owen continued, "I'm not really at liberty to say,"

"Hello, Owen." Sandra spoke up then, "I think I just gave myself away."

"Well in that case," Owen said, laughing again, "It was Sandra!"

"Sandra, I am honored." And it was true.

She and Sandra had a great working relationship. When Jacqueline had first come on board, she had wanted to prove herself quickly. She later learned that Sandra was trying to do the same.

Sandra hadn't been with the hotel much longer than Jacqueline, although she had been with the company for quite a long time. Sandra transferred to The Prenton Hotel from one of their sister hotels in London because The Prenton Hotel had been struggling. Now, in slightly more than three years, the hotel was leading the company in profitability, and the very process that caught the attention of Jane Smith, enough for her to use it as the basis for her second book, was now gaining Sandra and Jacqueline a great deal of positive press within their company.

Bringing her back to the reality of the conversation at hand, Owen had one more surprise for Jacqueline.

"And Jacqueline," he said, "We would also like you to be the guest of honor and speaker at our annual Who's Who in Belfast banquet in December. We hope the story of your success will help motivate the audience to reach their professional potential."

Now Jacqueline was speechless and sat there with her mouth open slightly, looking to Sandra for help.

"She'd love to Owen," Sandra said in the phone. "Please email us both with the details, and I will make sure she is there."

"Sounds great, Sandra," Barry said. "And congratulations again, Jacqueline. My assistant will be contacting you soon for your interview and photoshoot."

As the phone disconnected, Jacqueline looked her boss and friend directly in the eye and asked, "What have you done to me?"

She must have looked pitiful because Sandra started laughing and after a minute, Jacqueline joined in.

"Seriously though. Now I have to give a speech?"

"Yep," said Sandra. "It's part of the burden of success. But don't worry. I'll share everything I submitted about you so you can see why they picked you."

As she stood up to leave, she said, "Just don't let your ego run wild, or I'll have to rein you in!" Sandra started laughing again, and was still laughing as she closed the door.

A couple of moments later, still staring off into space, a familiar face poked her head in the door. It was the shock of bright green that first caught her attention as Jane Smith walked in smiling. As usual, Jane's hair colors were quite unusual. This time mostly white-blond with three different green hues on the right side of her face. They always made Jacqueline smile.

"Jane! I am so glad to see you!" Jacqueline said. "I thought you'd still be sleeping after such a big night last night!

"I couldn't sleep any longer," Jane said and sat down in the chair that Sandra had just vacated. "Jeff is still sleeping. I'll wake him up soon though for our Black Taxi tour."

"You just missed Sandra," Jacqueline said.

"I ran into her in the hall. She was heading to the kitchen about a delivery issue. We didn't get much of a chance to talk. But she did tell me that you had some exciting news."

As Jacqueline sat down again herself, she laughed. "I don't know if it's exciting or not, but it sure is news." At Jane's curious look, she continued. "Sandra nominated me for the Top 40-Under-40 list here in Belfast. And not only did I make the list," Jacqueline said ruefully, "But I am number one on the list."

"That is incredible, Jacqueline! Congratulations!" Jane said, gleefully. "So why do you look so miserable?"

That question made Jacqueline laugh again. "I have to give a speech about why I am such a success at some big annual banquet."

With each statement, Jacqueline made large arm movements, clearly illustrating her discomfort with such a prospect.

"Tell me more," Jane asked, and Jacqueline was too caught up in her thoughts even to notice the line that brought them both together in the first place.

"Jane, I am fine in trainings, but to give a speech about myself seems … a little ridiculous. I mean, after all, what's so special about me?"

Jane could see the struggle in her friend and had seen it in others many times before. It wasn't that Jacqueline didn't believe in herself. Most likely, Jacqueline didn't recognize how special she was. Jane wanted to handle this delicately.

"Jacqueline," Jane began. "What concerns you most about this? Is it the award, the speech, something else, or all of the above?"

"I don't know," Jacqueline responded. "This just seemed to come out of the blue. Don't get me wrong. I am very flattered that Sandra would nominate me and honored to be chosen. But I guess I don't understand why they chose me."

"Do you believe that the successes you have had here were flukes?" Jane asked, knowing this would get Jacqueline's focus back on the process rather than on herself.

"No!" Jacqueline replied, just as Jane thought she would. "I have worked hard here to make my training and development plans successful. I know that," she said a bit sheepishly.

"I must sound like a whiny child," Jacqueline said with a laugh.

"Not at all," Jane said, shaking her head slightly and smiling to ensure her friend knew it to be a truthful response. "But something is gnawing at you about this, and I want to help you get to the bottom of it."

Jacqueline was quiet for a moment. When she looked at Jane again, Jane could see she had found at least one answer to her discomfort.

"I suppose I feel a little like an imposter somedays." Jane quirked her head to the side in silent question, urging Jacqueline to continue.

"I know that I work hard, and I know my methods work. But there is nothing special or unique about any of the things that I do. What if I get up to talk about myself and my program and the audience realizes they picked the wrong person to give the award to?"

Now we're getting somewhere, Jane thought. She had experienced the same doubts herself from time to time.

"Jacqueline, why do you think there is nothing unique to what you are doing?"

"Jane, you are really sneaky with this *tell me more* strategy of yours," Jacqueline said, laughing. "But I get what you are asking. I know there are unique things that I am doing, and probably most unique is how I put them all together. Maybe I'm not giving myself enough credit."

Jane smiled, pleased that her friend could see the value in herself. "I would agree with that answer," Jane said, nodding. "And yes, I am working the *tell me more* strategy, mostly because it means nothing for me to say those statements to you first if you do not believe them yourself."

Jacqueline nodded her agreement and said, "But I still have no idea really how to put that into words to give in a speech. Where do I even start?"

"Now that," Jane said laughing, "Is something I can help you with. And I have a few other people I would like to introduce you to that may help you identify what truly sets you apart."

"I would love that!" Jacqueline said, smiling. Jane could see the relief already transforming her initial fear to dedication to the process.

"First things, first," Jane said. "We need the full nomination documents from Sandra!"

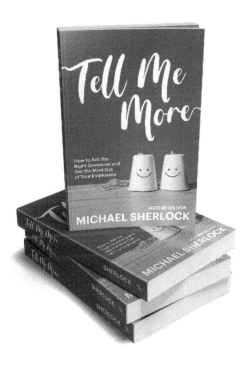

DID YOU MISS
TELL ME MORE?

Pick up a copy of *Tell Me More: How to Ask the Right Questions and Get the Most Out of Your Employees*, the first book in the *Shock Your Potential* series, today to see how Maria's story began, and to learn valuable methods and tools of the Listen, Learn, and Lead system to grow your leadership skills.

Tell Me More is available in paperback and Kindle editions at Amazon.com.

Made in the USA
Middletown, DE
20 January 2022